The 10X Financial Advisor

Your Blueprint for Massive and Sustainable Growth

Scott Winters

Absolute Author Publishing House
New Orleans, LA

Absolute Author
Publishing House

The 10X Financial Advisor
Copyright ©2020
Scott Winters

Publisher: Absolute Author Publishing House
Editor: Dr. Melissa Caudle
Interior Formatter: Dr. Melissa Caudle

ISBN: 978-1-951028-50-3

Winters, Scott/*The 10X Financial Advisor*

p. c.m.

1. Finance   2. Financial Services

DEDICATION

I dedicate this book to:

My Father George, who taught me to be a man.

My wife Jennifer, who completes me.

My six kids, Ashley, Kaili, Scott II, Zack, Samantha, and Drake who motivate me.

I love you all and will forever be grateful for you being in my life.

TABLE OF CONTENTS

FORWARD i

INTRODUCTION v

CHAPTER 1: EVALUATION 1

Stage One: Evaluation 2

ASN = Advisor Success Number 3

CIN = Client Interaction Number 3

SRN = Scale Ready Number 3

ASN Unveiled 5

Life Cycle of Client Engagement 5

ASN Case Study 10

CIN Unveiled...11

CIN Case Study 15

SRN Unveiled...16

SRN Case Study 85

CHAPTER 2: DIAGNOSTICS 88

Business Diagnostics 89

CHAPTER 3: WEAKNESS RESOLUTION 95

Taking Action 96

WR Case Study 98

CHAPTER 4: BUSINESS CONSTRUCTION .100

Business Construction (BC) 101

CHAPTER 5: CONFIRMATION 109

Confirmation (C) 110

CHAPTER 6: BUSINESS MODELING 118

Business Modeling & Scaling (BMS) 119

CHAPTER 7: EXECUTION and
ACCOUNTABILITY 129

Execution (EX) 130

Accountability (A) 132

CHAPTER 8: THE 10X CLUB 138

Welcome to The 10X Club 139

ABOUT THE AUTHOR 143

INDEX 145

REFERENCES PAGE 147

Wealth consists not in having great possessions, but in having few wants. - **Epictetus**

FOREWORD

*"Everybody needs money. That's why they call it money." - **David Mamet***

Helping clients achieve their financial goals is one of the most rewarding careers you can choose. The work itself is satisfying. There's no limit to the amount of wealth and security you can build for yourself, and you don't need to have a graduate degree, speak a foreign language, or know how to program computers, to do it. If your grandmother can swap Bundt cake recipes on Facebook, you can handle the technology you need to build a million-dollar business.

Unfortunately, financial services are also one of the most daunting careers you can choose. Every year, thousands of bright, ambitious new advisors get licensed, get trained, and get to work. The vast majority of them fail and fail surprisingly fast. It turns out that while advising clients how to make smart financial choices looks easy, building a business that actually gives you the privilege to do it is very hard indeed.

So, what separates the vast majority of wannabes from the elite group of what Scott Winters calls 10x Advisors? The answer is, the 10x Advisors have a plan to succeed by thinking like a business owner. They focus their time and energy on things that actually grow their business and avoid the temptation to waste time on shiny things that take their eye off of ultimate success.

In short, they follow the Quantum Leap formula that Scott reveals here in this book.

If you're looking to launch a new financial services practice or grow your existing business, you can't find a better mentor than Scott. He's done it himself, which is difficult enough, but he's also proven he can coach *you* to do it, too.

Scott's own track record would have been enough to satisfy many in the business. He has had a successful multi-decade career in the financial services industry as a top financial advisor, manager, and executive. Notable accomplishments are that he built a wealth management business from zero to over two billion in assets managed across over 20,000 clients. He co-founded, built and sold one of the fastest-growing wealth management businesses in America (according to Forbes).

Once Scott climbed to the top of that hill, he saw one even higher -- the chance to train advisors. He's used the lessons he learned developing the Quantum Leap formula for himself to train advisors across the country to achieve greater success for themselves and, ultimately, their clients. He has mentored, managed, or trained thousands of financial advisors and I am confident that he can help you build a stronger more competitive business. Scott has continuously rewritten the book on the use of technology and practice management disciplines to help achieve massive and sustainable business growth. The 10X Financial Advisor is a culmination of the experiences and lessons learned over a quarter of a century career.

Today, Scott's on a new mission as CEO of the Financial Gravity Companies, Inc. Financial Gravity owns and operating several financial services companies including a broker-dealer, a registered investment advisor, a turnkey asset management provider, and an insurance marketing organization. They also include FA Mentor, a training program dedicated to helping advisors take maximum advantage of the Quantum Leap program he outlines here. This program represents two solid years of work packaging his program to overcome the obstacles he saw so many advisors struggling with.

Scott has already built an enviable reputation among thousands of top advisors across the country. The Quantum Leap Formula and FA Mentor program represent his invitation for you to join them at "the grownups table." You won't just build a business you can be proud of to operate. You'll build a life you'll be happy to live.

Ed Lyon, JD
CEO, Tax Master Network

INTRODUCTION

So, you want to be a million-dollar producer or dare I say it, a multimillion-dollar producer. How do you get there? The simple answer is that you need a recipe. Many financial advisors toil in mediocrity for years haphazardly trying different ways to jump-start their business. They forge their path forward by feeling, or even worse by trial and error. They waste time, effort, and money, chasing every new idea, thinking that this time will be different. This time I will become the success that I always dreamed I could be.

Unfortunately, time and time again, you find yourself stuck in the cohort of the average. The good news is that you do not have to be average anymore. There is a model to build just about everything. If you want to build a house, you would be out of your mind to proceed without a blueprint. If you want to build a business, you can build a plan emulating the world's most successful companies. There is absolutely no difference in our business. If you want to be a financial advisor superstar, there is a model. This book is dedicated to providing every reader with a clear, understandable path to membership in the 10x club.

Building a successful financial advisory business can be broken down into a simple mathematical equation that anyone can follow. I know that a couple of sentences ago, I used the words "clear" and "understandable," so please bear with me as I lay out the math behind your successful business reincarnation. At first glance, it might appear a wee bit complicated, but I promise you it will make sense as I describe how all the pieces fit together.

Math, Science, and Business Intertwined
The Quantum Leap Success Formula

ASN+CIN+SRN=QLSN
QLSN+WR+BMS*EX= QLS

Now that you are completely perplexed, let us breakdown the individual components to our success model.

ASN: Advisor Success Number
CIN: Client Interaction Number
SRN: Scale Ready Number
QLSN: Quantum Leap Success Number
WR: Weakness Resolution
BMS: Business Modeling and Scaling
EX: Execution
QLS: Quantum Leap Success

I know, it still does not make sense, but I promise it will all come together, just keep reading and it will become crystal clear before you know it. Throughout this book, you will notice a theme of repetition. Trust me; this is NOT early onset Alzheimer's. There are certain key points, studies, and business principles that are so profoundly important to this process that I have chosen to reiterate them for dramatic effect. Let's get this adventure started by breaking down and analyzing each facet of the components above. The result will be a life-changing business transformation that will put you in a position to make your dreams come true. By the time you finish reading this book, you will possess the knowledge to build your very own blueprint for massive and sustainable growth. Welcome to the 10x club.

What is a 10x Advisor, and why do I want to

be one?

In almost every profession, there is a cohort of people that make up the best of the best, la creme de la creme. The rest of the surrounding people are left looking in with wonder. How did they achieve such fantastic success? How did they get to such an extraordinary level of talent? You could very well be talking about the computer scientist that can code ten times faster and more proficient than their peers or the salesperson that earns 10x more than the others. Almost everywhere you look, there are people who have broken out of the mold of mediocrity and go on to do something truly great within their respective spheres.

How about your company? At most financial firms, there is one, or perhaps a few individuals who are ten times more successful than all the other advisors. What are they doing differently than you? Has it ever felt like you work just as hard, but do not even come close to the same output?

The answer is quite simple; the 10x advisor has mastered the principles of business and applied them to their advisory practice. They have a solid business plan and emphatically execute. In other words, they have their own mathematical equation that they have built and follow religiously. By the time you finish reading the 10x Financial Advisor, you will possess the necessary knowledge and framework to challenge the status quo and complete for your own spot in the 10x club at your firm.

The Quantum Leap Success Formula is intertwined throughout an eight-stage process. The next several chapters will take you through a journey focusing one section at a time, through each of the eight stages, to create your blueprint for success.

The Eight Steps

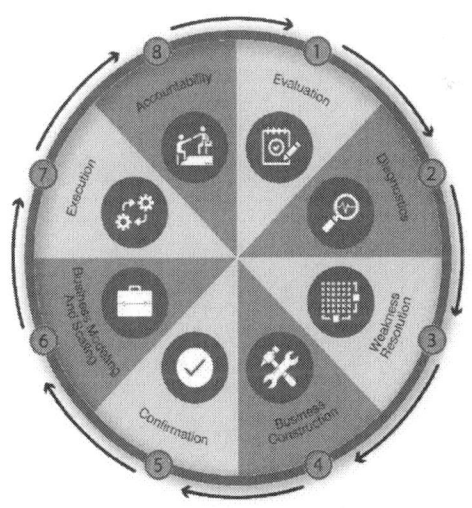

CHAPTER 1

EVALUATION

Every day is a bank account, and time is our currency. No one is rich, no one is poor, we've got 24 hours each day. - **Christopher Rice**

CHAPTER 1
EVALUATION

Stage One: Evaluation

You cannot build a magnificent building on a weak foundation. Think of the Evaluation phase as the foundation that your entire business is built upon. If you mess up this most critical stage, your entire business can come crashing down. Back to our math for a minute, the first part of our equation is to solve for QLSN. We

2

get there by adding ASN to CIN to SRN. Let's break those components down and later in this chapter, we will detail the importance of each piece.

ASN = Advisor Success Number

The Advisor Success Number (ASN) is the measurement of a financial advisor's strengths and weaknesses throughout the total life cycle of client engagement. A high ASN has shown to be statistically highly correlated with success and even superstardom, while a low ASN can be a launching point to resolve weaknesses and jump-start your career.

CIN = Client Interaction Number

The Client Interaction Number (CIN) measures the amount of time that you spend doing the things that actually make you money, creating relationships, and deepening relationships. In other words, prospect and client-facing activities.

SRN = Scale Ready Number

The Scale Ready Number (SRN) measures your readiness to take your financial advisory practice and scale it for massive and sustainable growth. The SRN takes into consideration all of the elements that need to be in place to turn your practice into a truly thriving business.

When you put it all together, your Quantum Leap Success Number (QLSN) is the sum of your ASN (your strengths and weaknesses throughout the total life cycle of client engagement) plus CIN (your focus on prospect and client interaction, and the ability to eliminate or delegate everything else) plus SRN (your readiness to scale your business).

Before we go deep into each of the three components of the QLSN, I want to lay the groundwork for why this exercise is so important. It all stems from ferreting out your weakness. If you can figure out what you are truly bad at or don't like doing, you can solve those weaknesses utilizing technology, systems, redirection of resources, outsourced marketing and lead generation. Please trust me when I say this, offloading what you are not good at is not difficult; the hard part is admitting that you have deficits. When you come clean with yourself, the end result is a business where you get to do the things that you love and are good at and you outsource your weaknesses. Your business will skyrocket and so will your happiness.

ASN Unveiled

As mentioned previously, the Advisor Success Number (ASN) is the measurement of a financial advisor's strengths and weaknesses throughout the total life cycle of client engagement. There are five unique steps in the client engagement life cycle. Each phase requires varying and different talents in order to be a master of that domain. It is very rare that an individual is a master of all five categories, and therein lies a huge opportunity. I will explain shortly, but first, let's categorize and define each of the five phases of the client engagement life cycle.

Life Cycle of Client Engagement

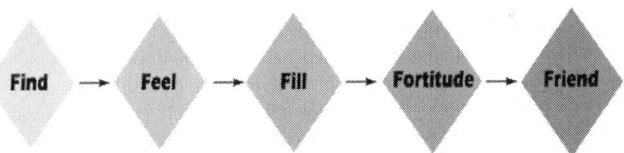

1. **Find--** The lifeblood of this business is the relentless pursuit of new clients. The biggest reason for failure or failure to thrive for a financial advisor is a lack of a new deal flow. It is critical to success that a financial advisor has a clear and

repeatable process to create deal flow. It is just as important that a financial advisor master the art of figuring out who not to talk to. If someone isn't a good prospect and we dedicate time in a business capacity to that prospect we are wasting our most valuable resource.

2. **Feel--** the financial advisor must have the skills to uncover a prospect's true pain point. Often a prospect will provide the financial advisor with their goals and objectives, but not offer the true underlying pain points. The issues that truly drive their actions. If the prospect doesn't have a pain point, they are unlikely to make a move regardless of how good you think your presentation went. It is the financial advisor's job to play an amateur psychiatrist in order to ferret out the prospect's pain.

3. **Fill--** Once the financial advisor has determined that the prospect has a pain point, the financial advisor needs to evaluate if they are capable of filling the client's need and resolve the pain through the use of either products or services. As I mentioned above, if the prospect doesn't have a pain point, they

really aren't a very good prospect. The same is true if the prospect has a pain point, but the FA doesn't have a way of solving the pain.

4. **Fortitude--** If a prospect has a pain point and the financial advisor can solve that pain point, you have a great prospect. During this phase, the financial advisor needs to display relentless fortitude in their continuous pursuit. Stay on this prospect like white on rice until this prospect becomes a client. Just because this prospect is now qualified, don't assume that the prospect is ready to make a move. Timing is everything and during this stage, and persistence pays off. It may take weeks, months, or even years of continuous follow-up and reminders of your ability to resolve their pain before the prospect will become a client. Successful financial advisors continuously drip on their prospects in order to stay top of mind, so that when the time is right, they are the first person thought of.

5. **Friend--** This comes down the Golden Rule, "Treat others as you want to be treated." Your client servicing model

needs to be well-defined so that you always provide exceptional service. Often your clients become part of your social circle. By friending your clients, you:

1. Have a client for life (which is extremely important being that investors tend to move away from the FA every seven years)

2. You will have a continuous source of new referrals. Clients aren't necessarily going to recommend their financial advisor to their friends, family, and loved ones, but they will bend over backwards to recommend a friend.

Each of the five stages in the total client engagement life cycle requires different skills. The advisor that loves prospecting may have an intolerance to client servicing. The advisor that is the master of client interaction and plan and product design may be terrible at finding deal flow. I have coached several advisors that excel at phase one (finding people to talk to), two (Figuring out their pain points), three (resolving the prospect needs) and five (providing exception service and friendship), but sadly their deficit in phase four (relentless pursuit) leads to massive lost opportunity.

To be a 10x advisor, you need to fill the gaps and make sure that the entire life cycle of client engagement is complete. By figuring out where your talent and passion lie within the five-phase framework, you will have an incredible opportunity to shore up your weaknesses utilizing technology, systems, redirection of resources, outsourced marketing, and lead generation.

Here is a simple example of a tool used to measure your ASN.

ⱯMENTOR Advisor Name: _____

ADVISOR SUCCESS NUMBER (ASN) QUESTIONAIRRE

1. How good are you at finding new clients (prospecting)?

    1 2 3 4 5

2. How good are you at feeling out the client's true motivation, goals and objectives? Finding the prospects pain points.

    1 2 3 4 5

3. How good are you at building solutions that properly fill the client's needs and resolve the client's pain points in order to help them achieve their goals?

    1 2 3 4 5

4. Once you have determined a prospects pain points and have adequately demonstrated that you can fill or resolve the client's pain, rate your fortitude in the eyes of rejection? In other words, if a prospect rejects your ideas do you give up easily or do you relentlessly pursue the prospect for weeks, months and even years to come?

    1 2 3 4 5

5. Do you friend the top 20% of your client's? In other words, do your best clients become part of your social circle?

    1 2 3 4 5

Download the tool at www.fa-mentor.com

ASN Case Study

Several years ago, I had an individual working for me; we will call him John Bilkinson. John was 30 years in the business, very talented, a hard worker, and had a magnetic personality. He was the kind of guy that would light up the room when he walked in. John was a master of phases one through four, and those skills led to a successful career. He would prospect

10

relentlessly and was very good at it. He was exceptional in client interaction and figuring out his prospect's pain points. He mastered the art and science around designing ways to solve the prospect's pain points. John was perhaps the most relentless pursuer of a qualified hot prospect that I have ever seen.

John was so tenacious that he would chase his prospect with calls, mail, email, drop by visits, etc. until the prospect either bought or told him to stop (usually with expletives). However, even though John was a success, he never broke out into the category of 10x. John had a constant churn. He brought in clients faster than anyone else in the organization, but unfortunately, he lost them more quickly than anyone else in the company. If John was as a talented at client servicing and creating friendships with the people that he served, as he was at all other phases of the life cycle of client engagement, he would have been a superstar. Find your holes and therein lies the opportunity.

CIN Unveiled

The Client Interaction Number (CIN) measures the amount of time that you spend doing the things that actually make you money, creating relationships, and deepening relationships. In other words, prospect and client-facing activities.

What percentage of your day do you spend doing prospect or client-facing activities? All too often, I see financial advisors work too hard and come away exhausted and still not find the results that they are looking for. The truth is that we only get paid well to do two things, create relationships and deepen relationships. Almost EVERYTHING else that we do is gross underemployment.

Imagine that you pick up your phone to make a doctor appointment, and on the other end of the line is your doctor greeting you with a "Hello." Then when you arrive at her office, she promptly hands you all the paperwork and insurance forms. She proceeds to photocopy your insurance card and then walks you back to the exam room, where she begins the exam by taking your weight, temperature, blood pressure, and documenting your reason for today's visit. After receiving professional advice and treatment, your doctor walks you back to the front counter, takes your payment and schedules your follow up appointment.

That is just crazy, right? I can't imagine that this doc will stay in business. The reality is that doctors are the kings of delegation. They have someone else perform all the things mentioned above except providing professional advice and treatment. By outsourcing everything else, they can run several exam rooms at the same time, seeing multitudes more patients and make more money. Why do so many financial advisors think that they get paid to manage money, create financial plans, do paperwork, etc.? I hate to break it to you, but these tasks are an underutilization of your skills. These tasks will not create the trust and loyalty of your clients that are so crucial to maximizing the client/advisor relationship, and without that trust, how do you expect your client to take your advice through thick and thin?

Rydex published a wonderful study regarding financial advisor's income levels based on the percentage of their time that they spent on prospect or client-facing activities. They found that advisors that spent more than 60% of their time creating relationships and deepening relationships made 8.42 times more money than their counterparts that spent 30% or less of their day on client-facing activities. That is huge!!! This is so important that I am going to repeat myself. That is 8.42 TIMES more money than the average financial advisor. Please, please, please, invest in technology, systems, people, outsourcing companies, etc. and stop doing the things that will not make you money.

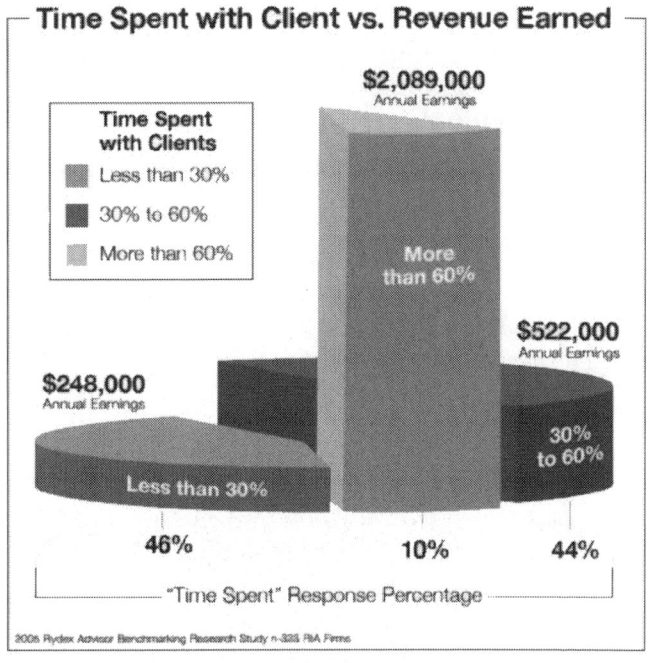

Time Spent with Client vs. Revenue Earned

Relentlessly measure and document every minute that you spend interacting with prospects and clients and chart it weekly. If that number is south of sixty percent of your entire work week, you are leaving money on the table. Learn from the techniques used by your doctor to scale and achieve massive and sustainable growth. Start treating your financial advisory practice like a business. Stop wasting your time doing $10, $20, or even $30 an hour work. You get paid well to create relationships and deepen relationships; now do it, and your business will explode.

Here is a simple example of a tool used to measure your CIN.

Download the tool at www.fa-mentor.com

CIN Case Study

Early in my career training financial advisors, I coined a term for the most common mistake I saw among average to failing financial advisors. I called it DAS. I observed that 85% of the time I could study an advisor's practice that wasn't meeting expectations and attribute the shortfall to the advisor catching a case of DAS. Okay, I know what you are thinking; DAS is not a next-gen venereal disease. In actuality, it is much worse. You can't just take a few doses of antibiotics and cure DAS. It takes education and a genuine desire to overcome your most powerful instincts.

DAS is short for Delusional Activity Syndrome. DAS is where a financial advisor works his or her fingers to the bone doing all the wrong things. To the outside world, they look super busy. In most cases, they even convince themselves that they are giving 100% of their time and effort to their career and attribute their lack of success to their bad luck. Remember, we get paid extremely well to do two things; create relationships and deepen relationships. Everything else is likely an underutilization of your time.

Let's look at an example of a $500,000 producer. If that advisor works 2000 hours during a typical year, she is earning $250 an hour. A Million-dollar producer earns $500 an hour. This advisor is leaving money on the table by doing anything that is less valuable than her personal average hourly value. Now, I know you may be thinking that your numbers aren't even close to these examples, but keep in mind if you want to be a 10x advisor, you need to think and act like a 10x advisor, or you will never get there. In my training days, I would walk the bullpen and you would see constant activity. Everyone looked busy, everyone was working long hard hours, but every financial advisor was NOT getting the same results. The advisors who spent the vast majority of their time on the phone or in the conference room with clients or prospects made their numbers. The advisors who spent their day doing other THINGS that they deemed important, whether it be organizing, or creating plans, or trading stocks, etc., failed. If you think that you might have DAS, please seek professional help immediately; your career depends on it.

SRN Unveiled

The Scale Ready Number (SRN) measures your readiness to take your financial advisory practice and scale it for massive and sustainable growth. The SRN takes into consideration the elements that need to be in place to turn your practice into a truly thriving business.

Ironically most financial advisors are really sh*ty business people. No offense, but it is true. They spend their days crafting plans and strategies to help their clients achieve their life's goals, but unfortunately, they fail miserably in planning for their own business success. After a quarter of a century in the financial services industry, managing, training, and mentoring thousands of financial advisors, I have seen it all!

I have witnessed some of the greatest success stories in our industry. On the flip side, I have had a bird's-eye view of the failure that is so prevalent in our profession. Most of the failure, or failure to break out into the cohort of elite advisors, stems from the lack of a clear and defined business processes and business acumen. Most advisors don't know how to run their practice like a business. They miss the basic business 101 elements that are essential to scale and achieve massive and sustainable growth.

To make sure that you are ready to scale your business, we are going to take an in-depth look at the following 21 items that are beneficial to achieving success and scale. Now that's not to say that if you don't accomplish every single item on this list that you can't be a 10x Advisor. However, most 10x'ers have mastered the vast majority, if not all of the items below.

1. Do you stand for something? In other words, do you have a clearly defined mission statement and value

proposition?

2. Do you know the demographics and population of your area? Have you done a competitive analysis of the market in which you compete?

3. Do you have a niche target market?

4. Do you consider yourself a specialist?

5. Do you have the proper tools and technology in place?

6. Do you have a sales and marketing funnel?

7. Do you spend enough money on marketing and do you calculate ROI on your marketing spend?

8. Do you do any social media or internet-based marketing?

9. Do you do center of influence marketing?

10. Do you have a multifaceted or multi-pronged marketing plan?

11. Do you survey your client base

quarterly using Net Promoter Score?

12. Do you have a client onboarding process?

13. Do you have a client servicing model?

14. Do you have a process for getting referrals?

15. Do you have a process for getting multi-generational client retention?

16. Do you do regular client appreciation events?

17. Do you send out a monthly newsletter or blog?

18. Do you have a full-time assistant?

19. Do you have an institutionalized process for managing your client's investments?

20. Do you have a process for firing clients?

21. Does your business have a personality?

1. **Do you stand for something? In other**

words, do you have a clearly defined mission statement and value proposition?

What do you stand for? In other words, what is your mission statement and value proposition, and why do they matter?

When I decided to write on this topic, the first thing I did was *Google* "financial advisor" in the county where I live. I was horrified. Of the top ten sites as listed on *Google*, not one of them clearly defined its mission or value proposition. What is even worse is that they were all so generic and whitewashed that they looked like a big chunk of cotton candy. Remember Marketing 101; you need to repel to attract. To make your words more relevant to your target market, repel everyone except the people that you specifically want to speak to. You should want to come across as the "Go to" professional in your market in the area in which you are an expert if you want to dominate that niche.

On the other hand, a mission statement that tries to speak to everyone does not attract anyone. It creates no identification of expertise and no differentiator. It will not attract a prospect to read beyond the six seconds that our attention deficit disorder culture allots to pique our curiosity enough to read on. It is a lost opportunity.

In contrast to the cotton candy, I *Googled* the website of some of the most iconic and successful brands like Intel, Uber, FedEx, Campbell's Soup, etc. and they all have a very similar pattern. They have a big, bold proclamation followed up by a two to five-part explanation of customer value. For example, Uber: "Get there. Your day belongs to you." The other three tenants are:

1. Easiest way around

2. Anywhere, anytime

3. Low-cost to luxury

Uber has brilliantly told us precisely what they do and the three benefits that they provide, and they did it in very few words (remember my ADD comment, the fewer words the better).

It is essential to understand the difference between a mission statement and a value proposition. Your mission statement should define "what" your company is and does. Your value proposition defines the reason why a client would utilize your services. Let's take a closer look at some of the critical components of each.

Your mission statement should explain the following.

1. What you do,

2. What makes you unique,

3. Your target audience.

Your value proposition should identify clear, measurable and demonstrable benefits consumers get when buying a product or service. It should convince consumers that this product or service is better than others on the market. In the case of Procter and Gamble, they say, *"Making your day better—in small but meaningful ways. We see big potential in life's little moments. Brushing teeth. Washing hair. Showering. Shaving. Caring for the baby. Cleaning the house. Doing the dishes, and the laundry. We make products that help make these moments a little easier."*

The aforementioned statements clearly describe their mission as making your life better, and they back it up with how they benefit the consumer by taking your daily chores and making them more manageable. Almost all successful brands take this approach. They tell you what they do and how it benefits you the consumer. My question is why are so few financial advisors trying to emulate such a successful and proven model?

Learn from the techniques used by "big business" to scale and achieve massive and sustainable growth. Start treating your financial advisory practice like a business. Make sure that when you present your offering to the world, you have clearly articulated what you offer, the uniqueness of your offering and the value that your clients receive from consuming your services. Don't end up looking like just another hunk of cotton candy.

2. Do you know the demographics and population of your area? Have you done a competitive analysis of the market in which you compete?

Remembering back to our early years of education, first, we learned how to add and subtract, and then we moved on to multiplication and division. Once we had a mastery of those concepts, the journey continued into fractions, decimals, algebra, statistics, geometry, calculus and so on.

Let's pay special attention to the progression of our educational road map. We did not start the process of learning in our very early years with the complex subject of calculus. That would have been absolutely absurd and would have almost certainly doomed our potential ever to learn the subject. We needed to understand and practice the fundamental building blocks before we could tackle something as complex as calculus.

The same is true about the demographics and competitive analysis within the geographic market in which you compete. These are your fundamental building blocks that need to be understood entirely before you can truly scale your business and gain ownership of the mind share of the communities that you serve.

When Proctor and Gamble releases a new product, they know exactly whom they are going to market the product to well before the item ever hits the supermarket shelf. P&G has done their research in order to take all of the impediments to a successful product launch off the table. They know what their potential customer's profile looks like including their age, wealth, region, gender, etc.

After they have a complete and clear picture of their target customer, they figure whom they are competing with for that customer's wallet. By knowing who their customer is and whom they are competing with for that customer, P&G can efficiently plan a product launch and a very targeted marketing campaign. They can take a rifle approach to their marketing efforts instead of a shotgun approach where they spray marketing dollars all over the place and just incidentally hit a potential buyer.

Obviously, by knowing the exact target, they can spend all of their marketing efforts and dollars in the correct venues talking to the exact person that they want to reach. This approach is infinitely more efficient and profitable than spending money to speak to an audience that may or may not have an interest in their product. With that said, do you know the precise description of your target client? Do you know your competition for your target client? Over the years, I have found that 9 out of 10 financial advisors can't answer the following questions.

1.   Can you describe the demographics of the people that live in the county or counties that you serve?

2.   Can you precisely describe your ideal client?

3.   How many people that match your ideal client exist within the geographic

area that you work?

4. How do you reach your ideal client?

5. What are the specific needs or motivations of your ideal client?

6. Who else in your market is targeting the same ideal client?

7. What are your competition's strengths and weaknesses?

8. What are your competition's marketing strategies?

9. What are the possible unmet needs that your competition is missing?

10. How are you going to differentiate yourself from your competition?

Until you can answer the questions above, you have no business spending money on marketing. Learn from the techniques used by big businesses to scale and achieve massive and sustainable growth. Start treating your financial advisory practice like a business. Emulate the practices of Fortune 500 companies. Know everything that you can about your target client and spend your marketing dollars wisely by talking to the right audience. Otherwise, you are only wasting your time, effort and money. Marketing by luck is not a recipe for scaling a business.

3. Do you have a niche target market?

You can't be everything to everyone, or you end up being nothing to everyone. Most successful businesses focus on a niche. Even Fortune 500 companies that have hundreds or even thousands of products will often concentrate each of their many products on a specific niche. Niche marketing is focusing all marketing efforts on a small but specific and well-defined segment of the population. Niche marketing is aimed at being a big fish in a small pond instead of being a small fish in a big pond.

In 2014, Levi's, concerned about declining sales in their 501 Jeans line, decided they would more narrowly define their target market and concentrate all of their marketing on that one cohort. Their target was 20 to 24-year-old white males and females, college-educated, with income in the range of $30,000 to $45,000.

These individuals are outgoing, driven, and a part of the upper class, Generation Y. Their target customer spends a great deal of time at live music events. The genre of music that these people listen to is rock, hip-hop, and rap music. They read *GQ*, *Men's Fitness* and *US Weekly*. They watch *ESPN* and shows such as *Breaking Bad*, *Mad Men*, *The Voice*, *Two Broke Girls* and *Modern Family*. A large amount of their time is spent engaging with friends and family via social media.

The geographic areas that they will target are urban settings like River North and the West Loop. These people shop at stores such as Macy's, Nordstrom, and Bloomingdales. WOW, that is pretty darn specific.

Have you defined your niche market as well as Levi's? Of all the financial advisors whom I have talked to over the years, I have only had one individual pass that test. Let's take a look at the three crucial elements of designing your market.

1. Figure out whom you want to work with. These people must have a need. You must have the expertise to fill their needs. It is an added bonus if your niche is centered around something that you are passionate about and love to do. I have seen advisors build their entire business around golf, wine tasting, charity, etc.

2. Describe your client. Know everything that you can about your niche and write it all down. How old are they, where do they dine, what are their likes and dislikes, what are their wants and needs, where do they spend their time, what media do they consume, etc.? The better you can paint a picture of your exact target the easier it will be to find them.

3. Make sure that you speak your niche's language. If you talk to most 70-year-olds about hip-hop, they will most likely tune you out. Take everything that you have learned about your niche and use it in your marketing, presentation, personal interaction, and EVERYTHING else that is client or prospect facing.

4. Stop trying to be all things to all people. Figure out whom you want to serve, learn everything you can about those people, and do a better job than anyone in your marketplace at filling your niche client's needs. Learn from the techniques used by big businesses to scale and achieve massive and sustainable growth. Start treating your financial advisory practice like a business. Levi's vastly restricted their audience to increase their sales. Become a master at serving your

niche and you will find your way into the 10x club.

4. Do you consider yourself a specialist?

Imagine that you get the heart-breaking news that you have a brain tumor and need to have surgery immediately. My guess is that you are not going to let your general practitioner cut you open and play around in your skull. That would be absurd. When your life is on the line, you want an expert — someone who has successfully completed the operation many times. The same holds true for almost every industry. I would not hire a bricklayer to paint my house. Our industry is absolutely no different. Let's explore five very important considerations when planning your specialty.

1. For a financial advisor to successfully scale their business, they need to have their mission and expertise aligned. It is essential that you have a compelling mission statement and value proposition. You need to tell the world what you do and the value that you bring to your clients. You MUST be a master of what you claim in your mission statement. If your mission is to help people retire, you damn well better be an expert in retirement planning. You need to have the consistency of messaging, action, and

client benefits.

2. People will see through you if you are a fake. If your subject mastery does not align with your claims, you will fail. The consumer is more educated today than at any time in history. The consumer of today will shop harder before deciding. If you do not speak the nuanced language of a master of your domain, you will be found out. If your prospect interviews two or three advisors before deciding, it will be obvious to them who can talk the talk and who is a fake.

3. Specializing in one domain will allow you to focus your educational journey. Let's face it; you cannot know everything about everything. Even if you tried this impossible feat, you would end up spending all your hours consuming education and there would be nothing left to give to your business. Learn everything you can about your area of expertise and outsource the rest.

4. By becoming a master of your domain, you will gain a reputation in your market. Most 10x advisors have a very narrowly defined mastery and they very effectively market that expertise. They

become known as the "Go to" person in their marketplace for those skills. A good reputation for being an expert will lead to people reaching out to you to solve their problems. Wouldn't that be a great feeling to have people tracking you down because they need your very specific help?

5. By becoming an expert, you become more referable. Most people tend to think in compartmentalized boxes. For example, if your client was talking to a friend about estate planning, and you are a generalist financial advisor, your name probably wouldn't enter your client's thoughts. On the other hand, if your clients know you have expertise in estate planning, they will immediately think of you when the subject of estate planning comes up.

It is time to align your mission and expertise. That is precisely what big business does. *Google* is known for its expertise in search, and they do it better than anyone else. Ben & Jerry's is known for its expertise in producing gourmet ice cream, and man that stuff is yummy. Most successful businesses have an area of expertise where they dominate their market. Most 10x'ers have an area of expertise where they dominate their market. Learn from the techniques used by big businesses to scale and achieve massive and sustainable growth. Start treating your financial advisory practice like a business. Figure out what you are exceptional at and rinse, water, repeat, over and over again. Do not try to be everything to everyone, do what you are good at and you will have to beat the new clients off with a stick.

5. Do you have the proper tools and technology in place?

When I started in the business, I was assigned a cubical, phone, phone book, and a dummy terminal on which I could look up quotes or news. Those were the days before electronic order entry. Remember those tubes that we would shove the handwritten order into and then place it in the hole in the wall? The vacuum sucking sound would hiss as your order flew up the wall and through the ceiling and into the cage for order entry.

Wow, I am dating myself here. Allow me to paint a quick picture of my surroundings. Imagine a bullpen of cubes where all of the neophyte advisors sat. We were surrounded by big plush offices that housed mostly million-dollar producers.

My first move as a rookie financial advisor shocked my office mates. I went out to the local electronics store and purchased a 486 computer. For those of you who do not remember the 486, that was the model before the Pentium was released. So, I took my new toy and placed it on my work desk and proceeded to load Act CRM 1.0.

Wow, the reaction that I got from the surrounding people was nothing short of astonishing. They made fun of me. One of the million-dollar producers told me to stop playing around with that fancy electronic box. Another advisor said to me that I was sure to fail out of the business if I did not start cold calling and stop worrying about my big calculator. Another advisor gave me a gift of a metal filing box with 5 by 7 index cards inside. He went on to explain that those index cards were the secret to keeping all the information about my clients and prospects, and the tool that he used to become a million-dollar producer.

In the face of constant teasing, I explained to my office mates that I was going to use my CRM to dig deeper into the hearts and minds of the people whom I serve. I was going to use technology to keep track of who I should be calling, when I should call, and most importantly, why. My foray into tech worked, and my business took off. I too was soon sitting in one of the plush offices surrounding the bullpen.

Fast-forward several decades, today some pieces of software are just absolutely indispensable if you truly want to scale your business. The CRM still reigns supreme. It is the brain of your entire organization. It is where all of your data is stored. It is a tool that you will use to measure so many of the important business KPI's that are crucial to running a successful business. Quick note-- Outlook is NOT a CRM. It is a glorified electronic phone book; it doesn't even touch the surface of the capabilities of a CRM. Another important tool for the 10x advisor is data aggregation.

High net worth clients want to be able to see a holistic view of their wealth by logging into one place. They do not want to have to remember seven, ten, or even more websites and credentials to check up on their investments. Besides, the elite advisors are already offering this service. If you are not, you are already putting yourself at a disadvantage right out of the gate. Next up is planning software. It is essential that you can understand your clients' future needs and then design a road map for them to attain their goals.

Clients need to understand the purpose behind their investments if they are to stay the course through good times and bad. Depending on the way that you manage your clients' investments, a good rebalance program will save you hundreds of hours (or more) a year. Please keep in mind that we get paid extremely well to do two things; create relationships and deepen relationships. Anything that takes you away from those two endeavors should be mitigated.

Because marketing is a core part of becoming a successful advisor, an email automation system is paramount. Your CRM may have these capabilities, but if it doesn't, find one and start using it right away. It will save you time and generate leads even while you sleep. The 10x'er absolutely needs a lead or form capture system. This handy tool will turn your website, landing pages and emails into a steady flow of new leads.

Imagine Walmart not having the systems in place to automate marketing, customer service, admin, inventory, etc. Without the proper technology, the company would implode. The same is absolutely true for your business if you try to scale without the essential pieces. Learn from the techniques used by big businesses to scale and achieve massive and sustainable growth. Start treating your financial advisory practice like a business. If you want to scale and become a 10X'er, make sure that you have the proper tools in place to make your business run like a well-oiled machine.

6. Do you have a sales and marketing funnel?

Have you ever gone online to research a product or service, only to find yourself bombarded in the weeks or months to come regarding that offering? I remember my first such experience being electronically chased around the internet. Early on in the digital marketing evolution, in the early 2000s, I started *Googling* for an internet-based screen sharing service that was cheaper than what I was currently using. Reading through the top ten search results, I read a description that looked promising, so I clicked on it. From that moment on, no matter where I went, that company stayed on top of my mind until I eventually subscribed to their service. The following is a progression of the relationship.

- I clicked on a banner that contained their advertisement.

- I received information that piqued my curiosity.

- They offered me a white paper regarding their service.

- I accepted the offer, and in return, I had to provide my name, email, and phone to get the goods.

- Seconds later, I had a white paper sitting in my email inbox.

- A minute later I was sent a thank you email from the salesperson covering my region.

- Ten minutes later, my phone rings.

Fast-forward five more minutes and I am on a product demo viewing the features of this wonderful screen sharing tool. Because of my skeptical nature, I did not buy right there on the spot, so the chase continued. Later that day, I went to my favorite website for news, and guess what I saw? There it was; a banner advertisement prominently popped up for that very same screen sharing service. Everywhere I went on the internet they found me. They were there when I arrived.

A few days later, I received another phone call

from the salesperson. A day later, I received an email comparing their features with the service that I was currently using. A couple of days later, I received a postcard in the old snail mailbox highlighting their value proposition. A couple of days later, the salesperson called again. This time I bought.

Two weeks later, I received an email asking me to rate their service, which I obliged by giving the top score. One week later, I received an email asking for a referral. They asked me (a happy customer) If I could recommend anyone else like me that might find their service useful.

As I author this book, you will find that almost every single Fortune 500 company has a process of creating awareness, nurturing the lead, closing the sale and asking for referrals. The process may be unique to each company, but the constant is that each company absolutely has an institutionalized process; meaning that every touch, whether email, phone, snail mail, re-targeting, etc. is orchestrated and automated. Every lead is handled the same way based on the actions of the consumer through an automated system. Nothing is left to chance.

Do you have an automated process that rigorously institutionalizes each and every touch that happens during the client engagement life cycle? Do you know at any given moment how many prospects you have in each stage of your sales and marketing funnel? If the answer is NO, then immediately call your CRM provider and ask them to demo their marketing automation and sales funnel capabilities. If they don't know what you are talking about, get a new CRM pronto. Learn from the techniques used by big businesses to scale and achieve massive and sustainable growth. Start treating your financial advisory practice like a business. Big business doesn't approach sales and marketing with a willy-nilly or randomized process, and neither does the 10x advisor. Every ultra-successful advisor has a well-defined and automated process that they have proven to be profit maximizing.

7. Do you spend enough money on marketing, and do you calculate ROI on your marketing spend?

How much money should you spend annually on marketing if you want your financial advisory business to grow?

Why did Coca Cola spend FOUR BILLION dollars last year on marketing? BTW, that colossal number represents 11.2% of Coke's entire global gross revenue. Coke is one of the most recognized names on planet earth. There may only be a handful of people alive that have not heard of this iconic brand. So, why continue to spend so much moolah on promoting a brand that everyone already knows? The simple answer is that they need to continue to spend money to stay on top of everyone's mind so that they do not lose market share.

The more pressing question is, why do so many financial advisors think that they do not need to spend money on marketing? The average advisor that does have a marketing budget rarely spends enough. It is quite interesting to *Google*, "How much should a financial advisor spend on marketing?" There is obviously a myriad of opinions, but the prevailing thought is somewhere between 2% and 10% of total annual gross production, with more of the "experts" leaning toward the 2% number. WRONG! WRONG! WRONG!!! I cannot say it emphatically enough; this is complete hogwash. If Coca Cola, one of the best-known brands, has to spend 11.2% of gross revenue on marketing, you should feel embarrassed to spend at a rate lower than them. After all, I am willing to bet that you have not established a brand in your community that parallels that of Coke.

According to a 2016-2017 Gartner Research study, companies are now spending roughly

12% of annual revenue on overall marketing. The industries with the largest spend are education at 18.5% and consumer services at a whopping 17.4%.

Wait a minute, did I just say consumer services companies on average spend 17.4% of their revenue on marketing? Hmm, are we not in a consumer service business?

Look, the reality is that you need to spend money to make money. Start slow; test your marketing to ensure that you have an acceptable RIO. Once you have established a proven process and conversion ratio, turn up the crank. After all, if I told you that I had a machine that if you put one dollar in and three to five dollars will come out the other side, how much money would you stick in that machine? I am guessing you would back up the dump truck.

Salesforce is a great example. They invest 49% of their revenue into sales and marketing! 49%! Think about that for a minute. That is nearly half of the $6.67 billion in revenue generated in 2016. What did they get in return for such a massive investment? They got growth! In 2016, Salesforce grew by 24% over the previous year. Learn from the techniques used by big businesses to scale and achieve massive and sustainable growth. Start treating your financial advisory practice like a business. Start spending money to grow your business, or you might find yourself on the wrong side of the cut line.

8. Do you do any social media or internet-based marketing?

In this day and age, EVERYONE is online, and if you are not, you are missing a huge opportunity. Even worse, you are probably conspicuously absent. The following statistics pretty much say it all.

Content marketing costs 62% less than traditional marketing and generates about three times as many leads. (Demand Metric)

Social media has become the most popular content marketing tactic reported by 90% of B2C businesses. (Content Marketing Institute)

How we consume information is different today than it was 20 years ago. We cannot expect to utilize the same marketing that we used a decade ago and get the same results.

Recently I was talking to a financial advisor

about his marketing strategy. For 12 years now, he has sent out mailers inviting people to a seminar to learn about social security planning. The strategy worked great for many years, but in the past couple of years, the results have dropped off dramatically. It is happening everywhere you look, the old gold standard for information delivery is becoming obsolete. Newspapers, once on every street corner, have almost completely disappeared. Television advertisements are far less effective than they used to be. A study by Arris, showed that 84% of respondents wanted to fast forward through the ads they watch, while 60% of them download or record shows so they can skip commercials. Now back to our two statistics on creating content that is shared over social media which is 62% less expensive and it generates three times as many leads. Wow, that is huge.

If you do not believe that the internet and social media are changing the landscape, ask Dell.

They are very strong on Social Media. They have a "Conversations and Communities" team of 40 people and engage in almost every major social media channel. They have several blogs, including a direct to consumer blog and several special interest blogs.

Some other Dell Highlights:

- They have over 65 corporate Twitter accounts

- They have more than 400,000 followers

- They do promotions on Twitter for example "15% off any Dell Outlet Inspiron laptop."

- They have sold Over $3 Million of merchandise via Twitter

Dell is not an isolated case. Every major brand is now entrenched in the fight for our eyeballs online. For more evidence, look back to our last presidential election. Hillary Clinton spent almost twice as much as Trump on advertising her candidacy and lost. Trump effectively used the internet and social media to disrupt the system and win the election.

The 10x advisors are already online. They are on *LinkedIn, Facebook, YouTube, Twitter, Instagram,* etc. They are posting content, re-posting other people's content and commenting on it, and creating a reputation within their social spear as being experts in their field. The Fortune 500 companies are taking advantage of every marketing opportunity that the internet allows, and so are the top tier advisors that you compete against.

Learn from the techniques used by big businesses to scale and achieve massive and sustainable growth. Start treating your financial advisory practice like a business. Get online today and build your reputation or you might find that you just cannot compete in the digital age.

9. Do you do center of influence marketing?

In 2017, Kim Kardashian earned nearly 50 MILLION dollars, largely by *Tweeting* and *Instagramming*. That's right, 50 million bucks just for voicing her opinion about products and services on social media. Mrs. Kardashian has achieved the ultimate standard of influencer marketing. Sprint has been active in influencer marketing. Not only did Sprint cause Verizon's famous "Can you hear me now?" guy to switch to Sprint, but the company has collaborated with musicians, entrepreneurs, and actors to gain the attention of a massive young audience. Many Fortune 500 brands are now playing the same game.

Now, I know what you are thinking, Kimmy probably isn't going to start *Tweeting* about your financial services business, but the good news is that there are a plethora of opportunities in your very own community to create an army of influencers that will flood you with prospective new clients. Here is a simple plan that you can follow to create your army.

1. Figure out who are the people in your market that have the ear of the prospect that you are looking for. The following are examples, but by no means a complete list, CPA's, tax attorneys, estate planning attorneys, insurance brokers, real estate agents, etc.

2. Create a list of all potential influencers.

3. Design a marketing plan to reach out to everyone on your list in multiple ways, social media, email, snail mail, phone, etc.

4. Explain to each person on your list that there may be an opportunity for a synergistic business relationship that may be mutually beneficial. Invite each person on your list for lunch to explore the opportunities.

6. At lunch, explain who you are and what you do. Make sure they understand your

mission and unique value proposition.

7. Before leaving lunch, ask for referrals to any of their clients that will benefit from your services.

8. Stay in touch with your army. Send them useful information every few weeks. If you have a newsletter or a blog, make sure they get it. Stay top of mind with your army.

9. Once you have started the process of creating a relationship, cultivate it. Take them to lunch once a quarter. Continuously remind them what you do and that you are there to help their clients.

10. Treat your influencers like gold because that is exactly what they are.

Most 10x advisors do precisely what I have just described. The 10x'er understands that they need to leverage their relationships to maximize their reach. The good ones have a core group of seven to ten professionals that each on average, refer one new prospect a month. That is seven to ten new prospects per month, or eighty-four to one hundred and twenty new prospects per year. Now that is a recipe for massive and sustainable growth. Now, don't get me wrong; this type of marketing is not a get rich quick scheme. It takes hard work and consistent marketing to find and cultivate your army. Once you have done the work, and your army is in place, it will pay dividends for years to come.

There are numerous ways that you can and should be marketing your business. Influencer marketing should be one of many marketing strategies that you should employ but is not your only path to building your business. Start building your army today and you will be one step closer to your spot in the 10x club.

10. Do you have a multifaceted or multi-pronged marketing plan?

In 2017, Pepsi's tone-deaf advertisement featured model Kendall Jenner as the leader of a group of protesters, who awkwardly mirrored the *Black Lives Matter* movement. After the campaign insulted the daughter of Martin Luther King, and created a mass social media backlash, Pepsi was forced to pull the advertisement and issue a groveling apology. This is a perfect example of why you need to diversify your marketing approaches.

Not all campaigns work, and not all campaigns that work, continue to work. I will give you a great example of the latter that was a little too close to home. Early in my career, I stumbled on a campaign that worked like gold. I would put one dollar in, and eight to ten dollars would come back to me. Obviously, with a payback like that, I did what any rational person would do. I dumped as much money as I could find into the marketing campaign, and the results were incredible. I was making a ton of money, so I doubled down; bigger office, more employees, more marketing, and it all led to more profits until it didn't. My golden goose marketing campaign worked like clockwork for over two years until it stopped. I was left with all of the overhead of a scaled-up business without a fall back marking strategy to continue to provide revenue.

Fortune 500 companies all have a marketing plan. Their plan consists of multiple channels and multiple campaigns across those channels. For example, a company's marketing channels might consist of TV, radio, social media, mail, email, referral marketing, etc. Their campaigns are the messaging that they used to motivate their target audience to take action. They diversify in both how they get their message out and what they are messaging. Most financial advisors fail miserably in achieving marketing diversification. They find one message and one channel and play it out until the diminishing marginal returns are so bad it is no longer profitable.

The 10x advisor will always invest their marketing dollars across multiple channels and messages. They will measure the ROI on every campaign. They will chart their ROI so that they can measure campaign profitability fall off. Just like Pepsi learned in 2017, the 10x advisor knows that not all marketing works, and they know how to pull the plug. Learn from the techniques used by big businesses to scale and achieve massive and sustainable growth. Start treating your financial advisory practice like a business. *Google*, Amazon, Intel, Apple, etc. would not put all their marketing eggs in one basket because they know that one misstep could be disastrous. Spread your eggs and find more baskets.

11. Do you survey your client base quarterly using Net Promoter Score?

You have probably heard the saying, "It is a lot more work to get a new client than to keep the one you already have." One of the biggest mistakes that I see the average financial advisor making is not dedicating the proper attention and resources to keep their clients happy. Do you really know your clients? I am not talking about superficial stuff like salary, net worth, etc.

I am talking deeper here. Do you know their true preferences? Do you know how they are feeling before they ever voice their opinion? Do you know without a shadow of a doubt that they are 100% satisfied with your service? Do you survey your clients?

Imagine a world where corporate America does not survey their customers. Without constant and measured feedback, how would our favorite brands understand the changing preferences of their user base? How would a CEO of a Fortune 100 company know when a product or service is no longer competitive in time to adjust? How would the product design team figure out what to build and deliver to the market? How would the management team know if they are delivering on their company's unique value proposition? Customer surveys are an essential tool in almost every facet of business success. Without this important voice, the operators of American businesses would certainly fail to live up to customer expectations.

Now that we have established the critical importance of the survey, I need to ask the 64-million-dollar question. Why are most advisors so arrogant that they do not think they need to get their clients' feedback? I have asked hundreds of advisors this very question, and I usually get a response that is some variation of "my clients love me, I do not need to survey them," or "I know my clients, and I know what they want," or (my favorite) "it is just too much effort."

I am going on record right here and now, that is a big bunch of hogwash. If there is even a semblance of truth to those excuses, then the average client retention in our industry would be substantially longer than six years. It wouldn't be the case that at any given moment in time, 35% of your clients are receptive to getting a second opinion from another financial advisor. The world that we live in is changing at a pace so rapidly that without a mechanism for regular feedback, you may wake up one morning to a practice that is suffering from Blockbuster Video syndrome.

Now that we have established that you need to survey your clients, here are some benefits that you might not have considered.

1. Surveying your clients will give insight into which clients are unhappy with your service and may be getting ready to move to another advisor. You may be afforded the opportunity to make necessary changes before your client makes the ultimate change.

2. Surveying your clients can help you refine your offering. Client preferences, along with environmental factors, are constantly changing. Make sure you find out what your clients need and want before they get it from someone else.

3. Surveying your clients can provide you with proof positive that you should stop wasting your time doing certain things that may be time-consuming and expensive yet provide very little client benefit.

4. Surveying your clients will let them know that you care enough to ask their opinion.

5. Surveying your clients will help keep you top of mind with the people that you serve and hopefully lead to better client retention and more referrals.

We have determined that it is critically important to have a venue for monitoring and measuring client preferences. We have also concluded that there are substantial benefits to be had for those that effectively open up the channels of communication with their user base.

Surveying your client in and of itself will not make you successful, many other aspects go into building a business, but not doing it might lead to failure. Learn from the techniques used by big businesses to scale and achieve massive and sustainable growth. Start treating your financial advisory practice like a business. Start surveying your clients quarterly right away and reap the benefits of happy clients, more referrals, and consequently greater success.

12. Do you have a client onboarding process?

You only get one chance to make a first impression. Client onboarding is the process of bringing on a new client to your business. It is your opportunity to build a relationship, address concerns, ensure they understand the services available to them, get the client up to speed, and start the relationship on the right foot.

Recently I asked an advisor, "What do you do when you get a new client?"

The answer that I got back was, "Well, I fill out the new account forms and send them in."

Wow, that is a terrible answer. There are dozens of things that need to occur to accomplish the stated mission above successfully. If you do not have a formalized process for making sure that EVERYTHING gets done correctly, you are bound to miss something. You are the shepherd of your clients' wealth — the sum total of everything they have spent their life working for. The client always needs to be able to trust you, and the last thing you want to do at the onset of a relationship is to provide any room for doubt. Moving to a new advisor can be scary. Transferring assets between firms can be frightening. Since the client is already in a heightened emotional state, you want everything to go perfect because if it does not you very well might lose that client. A client is three times more likely to leave during the first 90 days of a new relationship with an advisor, so you need to put your best foot forward.

Begin by creating a checklist of all the things that you are going to do for your client during the first three months of your new relationship. For example, a new account paperwork, risk tolerance questionnaire, client agreements, a new client intake form, etc. Put everything down, even the small stuff. The most minor thing can make a big difference. For example, make sure your client is on your newsletter distribution list, birthday cards are scheduled, thank you for becoming a new client letters, are sent, and introductions to your team, etc. Everything that comprises the first 90-day client experience should be on your checklist. It is common for a 10x advisor to have 75 to 100 items on their checklist. They know that it is imperative to wow their new client with the best experience possible.

The next step is to automate and or delegate everything on your list that is not client-facing. Your CRM should be able to handle most of the automation of repetitive tasks on your list. Your assistant should do everything else. All Fortune 500 companies have an onboarding process for their new customers. They know that they need to show value immediately and provide an exceptional experience right out of the gate or they will churn their new client right out the door. Learn from the techniques used by big businesses to scale and achieve massive and sustainable growth. Start treating your financial advisory practice like a business. Create a process and follow it and your clients will not only be ecstatic, but they will tell their friends about the exceptional service they received.

13. Do you have a client servicing model?

Almost all successful businesses have a client servicing model. They treat opportunities with greater revenue possibilities differently than opportunities with less potential. If you call Verizon and want to get a cell phone service for your 100+ person company, you have a completely different experience then the person calling to subscribe to an individual plan. Businesses need to parse out opportunities to increase revenue, and so do you. Creating your client servicing model is quite simple. Decide what qualifies your clients to be classified as either an A, B, or C client. You will generally use some determinants like revenue, AUM, number of referrals, etc. Then decide what you are going to do for each class of client. For example, you meet with your "A" clients twice a year, "B" clients once a year, and "C" clients you meet with virtually via WebEx. The face time is just the beginning. Your client servicing model should detail every touch. Include everything that you are going to do for your client, and when you are going to do it, across each of the three client classifications. Like I said earlier, creating your client servicing model is pretty simple. The hard part is sticking to it and consequently, that is where most advisors fail. I am going to detail out five reasons it is absolutely essential that you have a client servicing model and stick to it religiously if you want to be a 10x advisor.

1. Having a well-thought-out and defined client servicing model allows you to

allocate your time properly. Your "A" clients should receive most of your time and attention. If you don't keep your top clients happy, they will leave you for another advisor. Losing a million-dollar client will sting much worse than losing a client that generates very little revenue.

2. A client servicing model will allow you to set proper expectations with your client upfront at the onset of your relationship. If you take on a new client and know that they will be classified as a "B" client, but you tell them upfront what you are going to do and when you are going to do it, you have established the rules of engagement. One of the biggest reasons why clients leave their advisors is because expectations and reality did not match up.

3. A properly designed client servicing model will help increase your bottom line. When you define what you are going to do and whom you are going to do it for, you become acutely aware of where you are spending your time and what you are getting paid for your efforts. A multimillion-dollar account will generate substantially more revenue

than a $100,000 account and should get more of your time and attention.

4. A client servicing model will lead to happier clients. When expectations and reality align, you have happy clients. When you have happy clients, you get more referrals. When you get more referrals, you make more money.

5. Having a client servicing model that is well-defined and rigorously followed eliminates the guesswork and provides your staff with the rules of engagement. If your team knows what to do and when to do it, you will have happy employees and happy clients. Once again, happy clients lead to more clients and more money.

Every Fortune 500 company has a process for client segmentation. They define how each client fits into each segment and what level of service each of those clients receives. Why don't you? Learn from the techniques used by big businesses to scale and achieve massive and sustainable growth. Start treating your financial advisory practice like a business. Create your segmentation, define your service, tell your clients what you will do for them, and I promise you will have happy clients and more rewarding experiences for you and the people that you serve.

14. Do you have a process for getting referrals?

Have you ever purchased something either in a store or online and subsequently received an email nicely asking if you know anyone else like you that might have an interest in the same product or service? Of course, you have. Most Fortune 500 companies have a well-thought-out and automated way to ask their happy clients for referrals. Why don't you?

One of my favorite questions to ask financial advisors is, "How do you cultivate referrals?" Sadly, about 70% of the advisors that I ask shoot me back a response that is something like, "Well, I am not really that good at getting referrals."

My next question is, "Do you ask for them?"

The answer is almost always "No."

This one fact alone may be the single biggest mistake made by the non-10x'er. Let us take a quick look at how referrals affect a marketing budget. Let's say that the retailer needs to spend

$100 to acquire a new client. What if one out of every ten new clients recommended a friend? The first ten clients cost the company $1000. The eleventh client was free. That brings down the average cost of acquisition of a new client to $90.90. That is almost a 10% saving in the marketing budget. Because our business is so relationship-driven, the numbers start to get scary good for the advisor that becomes proficient at leveraging their clients for referrals. Suppose a $350,000 producer spends 12% of their annual GDC on marketing, which amounts to $42,000 a year. The marketing that this advisor has been doing has been averaging about $1200 per new client cost of acquisition. That is 35 new clients per year. Now, what if half of your clients gave you a referral? You just increased your new clients per year to 52.5 and decreased your client acquisition cost to $800. That is HUGE!!! And, that is without spending one extra penny more on marketing.

How do you get referrals? The first thing you need to do is stop treating your pursuit of referrals as a haphazard activity. Getting referrals requires a marketing strategy and should be treated like any of your other marketing campaigns. There are two classifications of the referral ask; either a passive ask or an active ask, and both should be utilized to maximize success. Let us break down the difference.

The passive referral ask is the text that you should plaster EVERYWHERE, that says something like, "Thank you for being a loyal friend and client. I really appreciate your business. Do you have a friend, co-worker, neighbor, loved one that could benefit from my help? Please take one minute and fill out the attached form."

I have seen 10x'ers place these words in the signature line of their email, website, on client performance reports, marketing materials, etc. They make sure those words are prominently displayed on everything that their client sees or touches. It's all about staying top of mind and constantly reminding your clients that you are there to help their friends when the time is right.

The active referral ask is when you just come out and ask for it. Create a campaign and run the campaign religiously. Here is an example of a campaign that works like gold. Send a client survey once a quarter using the Net Promoter Scoring system. If your client gives you a high score, indicating that they would recommend you to a friend, call them and ask for a referral. Ask for a referral at the conclusion of every client meeting. Ask for a referral when you do something extraordinary that pleases your client. Remember, if you don't ask you don't get.

Learn from the techniques used by big businesses to scale and achieve massive and sustainable growth. Start treating your financial advisory practice like a business. Fortune 500 companies continuously ask us for referrals. They do it via relentless and automated campaigns because they know that it will drive down their cost of acquisition and increase their bottom line. Remember, if you don't ask you don't get. Moreover, if you do ask, you will find yourself one step closer to the 10x club.

15. Do you have a process for multi-generational client retention?

Amazon spends nearly four BILLION dollars a year on marketing. Imagine spending that much dough and getting absolutely nothing for your hard work and a boatload of money. Fortunately for Amazon, that is not the case. They have consistently been one of the fastest-growing companies in America.

However, the exact opposite is about to become your nightmare. Over the years to come financial advisors are going to spend more money on marketing than ever before in the history of our industry. They are going to be forced to work harder and more hours than in the past. The reward for these extra hours and huge marketing spends is going to be (wait for it) NOTHING. Their business will stay flat.

There will be NO increase in new AUM whatsoever. On the bright side, that money and hard work should allow the advisor not to shrink so fast that their business goes away completely. Now before you think that I believe in a doomsday scenario for the financial advisory business, let me add in a disclaimer. Not all advisors are going to suffer this apocalyptic devastation. The top advisors will be rewarded handsomely. It is the poor to average producers that will suffer this terrible fate. The proof is in three well-known statistics.

1. Boomers control 70% of all disposable income in the United States according to *US News and World Reports*.

2. Two-thirds of heirs fire their parents' financial advisors shortly after they receive an inheritance, according to an InvestmentNews survey.

3. According to a study from the consulting firm Accenture, baby boomers have started to pass along their

life savings to their heirs, and this process will continue over the next few decades. When done, some $30 trillion will be transferred from one generation to the next.

Does it all make sense now? Your clients are going to die, and when they do, their kids are going to leave you. For every new account that you bring in, another one will walk out the door. Here is the unfortunate part. We all know what's coming. It has been well documented in the press. The industry has been talking about these demographics for years. Yet, when I asked (hundreds) financial advisors the question, "Do you have a process for multi-generational client retention?" almost every advisor that I have talked to said "NO."

The good news is that for the financial advisors that get ahead of the curve and start now by cultivating relationships with the next generation, the future looks exceptionally bright. We will have a Goldilocks window of time where you will have 30 TRILLION dollars up for grabs. The recipe to successfully navigate the coming Goldilocks years is really quite simple.

1. Build a relationship with the next generation immediately.

2. Leverage those new relationships for referrals so that you are well-positioned to take advantage of the world's biggest upcoming wealth transfer.

3. Work your ass off to grab as many new relationships as you can.

Money will be in motion like we have never seen before when we apply these principles. Learn from the techniques used by big businesses to scale and achieve massive and sustainable growth. Start treating your financial advisory practice like a business. I can guarantee you that Amazon and most other successful businesses are already putting plans in place for the next generation, so they do not find their offerings obsolete. Start now; the future is already here.

16. Do you do regular client appreciation events?

You walk in the office, pour yourself a piping hot cup of *Joe*, with a smile on your face you sit down at your desk to start want you believe is going to be a beautiful day. Then like a ton of bricks, it hits you deep down in your gut. As you read through your client updates, you realize that your client of 15 years just ACATed out their account. What is even more soul-crushing is this couple who you have loyally served for a decade and a half, did not have the decency to tell you that they were going to leave. At this point, your head is spinning. "What did I do wrong?"

The answer is pretty simple, and it is probably not what you expect. Most advisors jump to the conclusion that the client must have been dissatisfied with their service. Wrong! Wrong! Wrong!

Next, they will conclude that their poor unsuspecting client must have been lured away by some slick-talking competitor that promised them the world. Wrong! Wrong! Wrong, AGAIN! According to the Rockefeller Group, 68% of clients leave because they don't believe you care about them. Wow, that is an amazing statistic.

What is even more incredible is that this considerable lever for client attrition is entirely within our control. Now at this point, you might be thinking to yourself, "Wait a minute here, I have sent my client a Hallmark card for every major holiday and birthday for as long back as I can remember."

I am here to tell you that it is nice, but not a

substitute for face to face bonding. My dentist sends me Christmas cards; I really don't give a sh*t. If anything, it annoys me that I took the time to open something that was obviously mass-produced and sent without any real thought or consideration of who I am as a person. Client appreciation events, on the other hand, provide you with an opportunity to create shared experiences with your clients, and even more important, develop a sense of community.

Client appreciation events bring tremendous value to your business in a variety of ways.

- They build engagement
- They are a great way to express gratitude for your clients
- They create happy clients, which leads to a greater possibility of referrals
- They boost you and the company's credibility
- They increase brand awareness
- They allow your clients to see you as a human rather than just a service
- They create loyalty – who would want to

leave a business that treats clients well?

- You can create valuable insight into your business– ask your clients what they like and do not like about service and record it!

The most successful client appreciation event allows the client to bring a friend. Think about how powerful this is and the opportunities that it creates. While you are solidifying your relationship with your client, you are simultaneously building a new relationship with a potential new client. Learn from the techniques used by big businesses to scale and achieve massive and sustainable growth. Start treating your financial advisory practice like a business. I can guarantee you that almost every Fortune 500 company has a plan in place to reward its top clients and make them part of their community. When you *Google* "Corporate event planning companies," you get 393,000,000 results. Wow, that is a pretty gigantic number. That is proof in my book.

17. Do you send out a monthly newsletter or blog?

Do you currently have an effective drip system

to cultivate prospects and turn them into clients? A monthly newsletter or blog can be a great way to stay top of mind with your prospects so that they think of you first when the timing is right.

The following story is not about financial services but is still extremely relevant.

I knew that I needed a new SUV. My old one was getting a little long in the tooth, and the mounting deferred maintenance would be costly. I had convinced myself it was time to pull the trigger. Like any rational consumer, I went to my trusty computer to study my options. I even went to a handful of dealerships to take in that new car smell. Fourteen months later, I was the proud owner of a new SUV. So, I knew that I needed a new automobile. Why did it take me so long to make it happen? I will discuss my obvious procrastination in a few minutes, but first, I want to point out the incredible mistakes made along my 14-month journey.

These tragic mistakes were not made by me, these atrocities were committed by the several car dealerships that I visited. At each visit, it was the same movie. I walk in the door and overeager salespeople molested me. Before taking a test drive, they photocopied my license and took down personal information. Upon arriving back at the dealership, the hard sell starts. As the dance continues, the salesperson realizes that I am not going to help him meet his quota today, and he politely dismisses me so that he can move onto his next mark. Game over, I never heard another word from the car salesperson or the dealership.

This was not an isolated experience; it happened at every single dealership that I graced with my presence. The travesty is that if someone had continued to stay in my face by calling, emailing, sending letters, and staying top of mind, I probably would have bought from them. As it stands, no one really differentiated themselves. No one earned my business.

As sad as my car story is, I see that exact same fatal error committed daily by the average financial advisor. They visit with a prospect, get to know them, analyze their investments, maybe even produce a financial plan, and then when the prospect doesn't sign on the dotted line, the advisor forgets that the prospect exists. To understand the gravity of this mistake further, let us look at the psychology of consumer decision-making behavior. The consumer will take a journey across five distinct phases.

1. Problem/Need Recognition

2. Information search

3. Evaluation of alternatives

4. Purchase decision

5. Post-purchase evaluation

In my case, I clearly went through the first three phases of the buying process. I recognized that I needed a new SUV. I scoured the internet for information. I then visited several dealerships to evaluate my alternatives. Yet, I did not buy it. I procrastinated because the pain of going through the car buying process was greater than the pain, I realized by driving a less than stellar ride; UNTIL IT WASN'T.

For me, that day came fourteen months later. The same is true for your prospects. Once you have figured out your prospect's true pain points and come up with a solution to solve their financial problem, it now just comes down to timing. Just because you are ready to sell does not mean your prospect is ready to buy. Drip, drip, drip and keep dripping until your prospect becomes your client. Utilize a good customer relationship management system (CRM) and use it religiously. Send your prospects a monthly newsletter or blog post that provides them with useful information. Call with ideas. Do whatever you can to differentiate yourself and stay top of mind so that when the day comes that your prospect is ready to pull the trigger, you are the first person that enters their gray matter. If you don't, you are just giving away potential new clients and burning time, effort and money.

Learn from the techniques used by big businesses to scale and achieve massive and sustainable growth. Start treating your financial advisory practice like a business. Create a plan to continuously get your name and content in front of the people that you want to serve, and your business will prosper.

18. Do you have a full-time assistant?

Imagine the day in the life of a Fortune 500 CEO. She works from a massive executive corner office overlooking the beauty of the surrounding landscape from the top floor of a very tall skyscraper. Her schedule is usually packed from the moment that she arrives at work until she takes that last step to leave the building at the end of the day. She makes important decisions every day that have the potential to positively or negatively impact the lives of thousands of people that her company employs, not to mention the millions of shareholders that have invested in her company's stock. Her social life is glamorous and filled with hobnobbing with the rich and famous.

On one random Wednesday, as the clock strikes 2:00 p.m., she stands up from her desk, takes a stretch, bends over grabs the overflowing trash can and walks toward the elevator, goes down 32 flights and across the parking lot to the building refuge center and she finds there the destination for her waste. On her walk back to the building, she finds a maintenance closet and decides to take a quick mop around the lobby before returning to the 32nd floor. On her journey back, she notices a buzz of chatter coming from the very large bullpen that houses the company's internal sales team. *Why not?* she says to herself, so she sits down in one of the cubes and starts making outbound sales calls. After realizing that she does not have what it takes to be successful on the phones, she heads over to the file room and files one report after another until the mountain of paperwork is gone. After a visit to both the accounting and legal departments, she heads home for the day.

Does this story sound familiar, well it should? This is exactly how most financial advisors run their business. They do everything and consequently end up doing nothing exceptional. You are the CEO of your financial services company. Your time should be worth several hundreds of dollars an hour. STOP DOING $10, $20, $30, even $50 an hour work. It is a waste of your most valuable resource, your time.

Scalability is a characteristic of a system, model, or function that describes its capability to cope and perform well under an increased or expanding workload or scope. A system that scales well will be able to maintain or even increase its level of performance or efficiency even as larger and larger operational demands test it. How the heck are you going to be able to accomplish that without help? If you want to scale your business and become a 10x advisor, you need to act like a CEO. Imagine the CEO of Google or Intel answering their own phone, or even managing their own schedule. Don't even think about scaling your business until you have the support staff in place to allow you to dedicate your full attention to the two things that you actually get paid well to do, create relationships and deepen relationships. Learn from the techniques used by big businesses to scale and achieve massive and sustainable growth. Start treating your financial advisory practice like a business. You cannot do it all, so focus on your core competencies and delegate everything else and you will be on your way to punching your ticket to the 10x club.

19. Do you have an institutionalized process for managing your client's investments?

At this point in the book, you probably think I sound like a broken record when I say, "We get paid exceptionally well to do two things; create relationships and deepen relationships." Everything else is taking you away from those two most important activities.

The mistake that I see the average advisor makes time and time again is that they manage every single client differently. Image an advisor with 150 clients, which works out to approximately 450 individual accounts. If all 450 accounts are managed separately with different investments and varying percentages, you have one big colossal time suck on your hands. Almost every client can fit into one of five portfolios along the risk continuum from conservative to aggressive.

Create your five asset allocations and then slot everyone into the appropriate model. If there is a change needed to one of the models, you can create one order that effects all accounts subscribed to that asset allocation. An even better idea is to utilize the services of a turnkey asset management platform (TAMP). A TAMP will take away all of the headaches of managing client money and provide your business with a high level of professionalism

As mentioned earlier, most advisors manage a mishmash of different constituents and when they decide that they no longer like a mutual fund, or manager, or an individual investment, they have to sift through every single account and manually trade each. Wow, what a waste of time.

Remember, time is money. Stop wasting both. Fortune 500 hundred companies are the masters of process. They are so large and diverse that they need to create a process for anything repetitive. Imagine Microsoft sending out a different email to every customer when they subscribed to *Outlook* online. That would be absurd.

Now, imagine Uber having a different onboarding process for each of their 3 million drivers. That just would not have worked; the company would have failed.

So, why do you manage a mishmash book of business? Learn from the techniques used by big businesses to scale and achieve massive and sustainable growth. Start treating your financial advisory practice like a business. Move all of your clients into an appropriate model and watch your business grow.

20. Do you have a process for firing clients?

Okay, now we are getting into some pretty weird territory. Up until now, we have been talking about growing a financial advisory business through the acquisition of new clients. So, why would we want to do something so contra and destructive as firing a client? Let us discuss the principle of addition through subtraction, but first, here is a fun story that will bring this whole concept center stage.

On June 29th of 2007, Sprint sent a letter to approximately 1000 clients giving them the ax. That's right. They told them to take a hike. "You all are FIRED!"

For about a year, the wireless-service provider had been tracking the number and frequency of support calls made by a group of pain in the ass customers. As a Sprint spokeswoman told Reuters in July, "In some cases, they were calling customer care hundreds of times a month... on the same issues, even after we felt those issues had been resolved."

Ultimately, Sprint decided that by jettisoning these time-consuming annoyances that they would have more resources available to provide better customer services to their better behaving phone subscribers. They felt that by providing better service that they would create more customer loyalty and reduce attrition. Guess what? This is absolutely true in your business as well.

There are two reasons why you should fire a client.

1. They suck the life out of you. Your time is your most valuable resource, do not waste it. Do not let one client deplete the aggregate level of service that you provide across your entire client base.

2. The second reason to fire a client is that you have too many clients. Most advisors can manage approximately 150 households.

Depending on your staff and the hours you keep, it may be more or less. But the point is that there are a finite number of people that you can serve and still provide exceptional service. You have one hundred and fifty seats on your bus.

When client number 151 shows up at your door, you need to have someone find a new ride or your aggregate level of service for all your clients will suffer. Maybe you bring on a junior advisor to absorb some of your passengers that can't afford a full-price ticket, or maybe you pull the trigger and just let them go.

Learn from the techniques used by big businesses to scale and achieve massive and sustainable growth. Start treating your financial advisory practice like a business. Define your service levels and make sure that your clients fit.

Determine how many households you can successfully manage and still provide the people that you serve with the necessary love and attention that will keep them clients for life.

Addition through subtraction is a process that all successful businesses employ. Know whom you are going to serve, how much you are capable of serving, and serve it up better than anyone else.

21. Does your business have a personality?

"To me, business isn't about wearing suits or pleasing stockholders. It's about being true to yourself, your ideas, and focusing on the essentials." –Sir Richard Branson, CEO of Virgin Group

In business, there is nothing more important

than being authentic. If your business does not have a personality, it damn well better find one.

More importantly, it better match yours. According to *Wikipedia*, business culture is defined as:

> ...*culture* encompasses values and behaviors that contribute to the unique social and psychological environment of a business. The organizational culture influences the way people interact, the context within which knowledge is created, the resistance they will have towards certain changes, and ultimately the way they share (or the way they do not share) knowledge. Organizational culture represents the collective values, beliefs and principles of organizational members. It may also be influenced by factors such as history, type of product, market, technology, strategy, type of employees, management style, and national culture. Culture includes the organization's vision, values, norms, systems, symbols, language, assumptions, environment, location, beliefs, and habits.

Sir Richard Branson has created a culture-changing the status quo. He is quoted as saying, "Don't sweat it: rules were meant to be broken."

Google is well-known for its employee-friendly corporate culture. It explicitly defines itself as unconventional and offers perks such as telecommuting, flextime, tuition reimbursement, free employee lunches, and on-site doctors.

LinkedIn's company culture focuses on five main pillars – Transformation, Integrity, Collaboration, Humor, Results.

All three companies have vastly different cultures, yet they are all enormously successful. Your culture is your identity. Your culture doesn't have to look or feel like anyone else's. Your company personality must reflect you as a person.

It is the personality of your business. So, you might be wondering, "Why is it important that my business has a personality."

There are at least two main reasons.

1. You absolutely must hire people that can get behind you as a leader and your mission with a religious fervor. Without a mission your employees see you as nothing but a paycheck. If your company is void of a personality, it is all but impossible for your employees to find meaning and true fulfillment in their work. Consequently, you will have constant employee churn which will lead to a reduced level of customer service, higher training costs, and higher client attrition.

2. Your clients work with you because they are attracted to your personality and view of the world. There is an entirely different type of person that is attracted to Sir Richard Branson's personality than would be attracted to Tim Cook, the CEO of Apple. Personalities of people or businesses are rarely interchangeable. Trying to make a culture shift can have devastating consequences that can offend and drive away the people that made you successful in the first place.

Once upon a time, there was a RIA that had a visionary, scrappy, work hard play hard leadership team. They embraced their employee base and set out to change the landscape of financial services. This company became hugely successful. They grew mightily for over ten years until they crashed and burned.

This company "jumped the shark" when it brought in the Harvard MBA's in pursuit of faster growth. In their infinite wisdom, the Harvardian's put in place a boring, uninspired, non-visionary management team. There was a clash in cultures that drove away employees and clients alike.

Nothing destroys a company faster than killing its personality and offending the people that were attracted to it in the first place. Learn from the techniques used by big businesses to scale and achieve massive and sustainable growth.

Start treating your financial advisory practice like a business.

Every GREAT business has a personality that attracts an employee and user base. Stay true to your culture, embrace your own unique personality, and be authentic and you will find your way the 10X land.

Here is a simple example of a tool used to measure your SRN.

A MENTOR Advisor Name: _____

SCALE READY NUMBER (SRN) QUESTIONAIRRE

1. Do you have a mission statement? ___Y or N___, If yes, what is it?
_____

2. Do you have a clearly defined value proposition? ___Y or N___, If yes, what is it?
_____
_____

3. Describe the demographics and population of your area:
_____
_____
_____
_____

4. Who is your biggest competitor (Advisor) in your immediate area?

5. What is your biggest competitor doing to market themselves?
_____
_____
_____

6. In the eyes of people within your surrounding area, do you own the market? ___Y or N___
7. Do you have a niche target market? ___Y or N___, If yes, what is it?

8. Do you consider yourself a generalist or a specialist? _____
9. If you consider yourself a specialist, what is your specialty? _____
10. Do you do comprehensive financial planning? ___Y or N___.
11. If yes, what planning software do you use? _____

Download the tool at www.fa-mentor.com

SRN Case Study

In the early 2000s, I started working with a revolutionary new custodian. On the surface, they had a value proposition unlike anything in the market. They married technology with custody and clearing in ways that our industry had never seen before. I remember dreaming of all the ways that this offering was going to enhance my business, reduce my technology costs and eliminate manual effort.

When I tell you that this custodian was ahead of the game, that is the understatement of the century. They were 15 years ahead of the next closest competitor. From a technology perspective, they were absolutely killing it. The problem is that they were not ready to scale.

Their unique value proposition led to some immediate success, which in my opinion, led to their downfall. They did not put the systems in place to support their client base properly. They did not set up the proper marketing to take advantage of the PR that they received. They did not have the people in place to provide good customer service.

If this company had scaled appropriately, they would have owned the industry today. Instead of seeing the name Schwab on the side of towering skyscrapers, you would see their name. Unfortunately, today they are still relatively unknown, and even worse, they have lost their technology edge.

The moral of this story is to make sure you are

ready to scale your business. Do not try to wing it as you go. Being unprepared for growth is a recipe for failure.

CHAPTER 2

DIAGNOSTICS

I have not failed. I've just found 10,000 ways that won't work. - **Thomas Edison**

CHAPTER 2
DIAGNOSTICS

Business Diagnostics

Remember the first part of our success equations: **ASN+CIN+SRN=QLSN?**

Advisor Success Number + Client Interaction

Number + Scale Ready Number = Quantum Leap Success Number.

When you put it all together, your Quantum Leap Success Number (QLSN) is the sum of your ASN (your strengths and weaknesses throughout the total life cycle of client engagement) plus CIN (your focus on prospect and client interaction, and the ability to eliminate or delegate everything else) plus SRN (your readiness to scale your business).

We have free tools available on www.fa-mentor.com that will help you to determine your exact score.

During the Diagnostics phase, we take everything that we learned during the Evaluation phase, and we clearly outline your strengths, opportunities and weaknesses. This process focuses on understanding your strengths and documenting your weakness, which helps drive your opportunities for massive and sustainable growth.

In our FA Mentor Coaching program, we use a one-page tool that allows for a clear expression of the essence of your current business evaluation.

Here is a simple example of a tool used to measure your Strengths, Weaknesses and Opportunities.

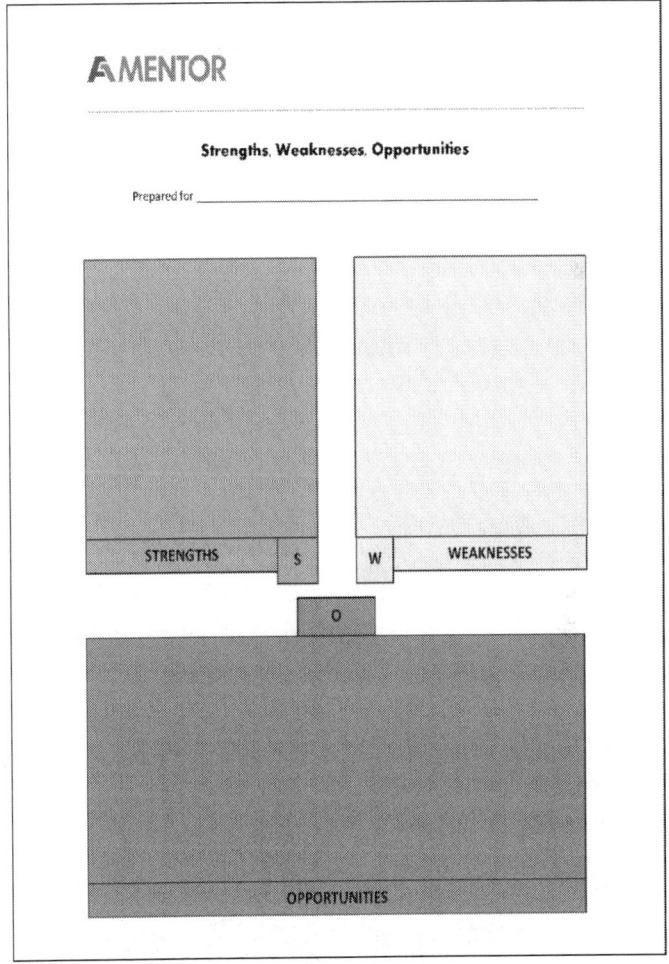

Download the tool at www.fa-mentor.com

I like to refer to this step in the process as the moment of truth. If you lie to yourself during this critical stage in the game, everything else from here on out is a waste of time. This one-pager is your gut check to make sure that your evaluation was done correctly, and you now have a solid foundation on which to build a business. Let us take a closer look at each of the three components of your moment of truth diagnostic.

Strengths: These are the areas in which your unique talents intersect with your business. Most importantly, these are the parts of your business that you probably enjoy and get the most satisfaction from. Most people enjoy doing things that they are good at accomplishing. This is an important lever for your success. If you enjoy what you are doing, you do more of it, and consequently, you attain greater success.

Weaknesses: These are the parts of your business that you are innately not good at performing. Remember the Bobby McFerrin song, *Don't Worry, Be Happy*? Don't worry that you are below par at some aspects of your business; this is your opportunity to rejoice.

If you are honest with yourself and embrace your weaknesses, there is a tremendous opportunity for three extremely positive outcomes.

1. If you stop doing the things that you are bad at your quality of life will improve dramatically. No one wants to go home at the end of a long day of work with a feeling of inadequacy.

2. By understanding your weaknesses and truly owning them there is an opportunity to outsource your frailties through technology, systems, redirection of resources, or complementary employees or partners. Stop doing the things that make you miserable and you, the surrounding people, and your business will all benefit.

3. By creating a better, enjoyable work environment and outsourcing the things that you are bad at, your business will take off and grow like crazy. Your prospects and clients want to work with someone that has confidence in their abilities and is happy in their own skin. If you are at peace and feel like a winner, that will come across in every interaction. Your confidence, coupled with a better client experience from outsourcing your weaknesses, will become a driving factor on your path to

becoming a 10X advisor.

Opportunities: This is quite simply your strengths minus your weaknesses plus the business 101 elements that you neglected to incorporate. Do more of the things that you are good at and stop doing the things that you suck at. In each of the three areas of evaluation, ASN, CIN, and SRN figure out what you either like doing, don't like doing, or aren't doing at all, and fill the gaps with technology, systems, outsourcing, and your business will thrive.

CHAPTER 3

WEAKNESS RESOLUTION

It is our choices, that show what we truly are, far more than our abilities.
– J. K. Rowling

CHAPTER 3
WEAKNESS RESOLUTION

Taking Action

Now that we have documented our strengths, weaknesses, and opportunities, it's time to start taking action. The next step in the process is solving for the holes in your business.

In the Weakness Resolution (WR) phase, you should develop an action plan to outsource your weakness through technology, systems, redirection of resources, outsourced marketing, and lead generation.

Remember, it is time to stop trying to get

better at your weaknesses and focus your energy on what you are really good at. At FA Mentor we use the following action plan to detail our list of tactical steps towards your journey to 10X status.

Here is a simple example of a tool used to create your Action Plan.

Download the tool at www.fa-mentor.com

WR Case Study

Earlier in this book, I wrote about an individual named John Bilkenson. John was exceptional in client interaction and figuring out his prospect's pain points. He mastered the art and science around designing ways to solve the prospect's pain points. John was perhaps the most relentless pursuer of a qualified hot prospect that I have ever seen. He was so tenacious that he would chase his prospect with calls, mail, email, drop by visits, etc. until the prospect either bought or told him to stop. However, even though John was a success, he could not break out into the category of 10x. John had a constant churn. He brought in clients faster than anyone else in the organization, but unfortunately, he lost them more quickly than anyone else in the company, until we solved for his weakness.

Once the problem became apparent, we teamed John up with a young lady who was exceptional at nurturing his client base. This lady was not good at any of the things that John excelled at doing.

If she were left to her own devices, she would have surely failed out of business faster than

you   could   say,
"*supercalifragilisticexpialidocious*" three times.
However, together they were gold. Together
they were complete and beautifully crushed all
five areas of the life cycle of a client
relationship. Together they became a 10X'er.
That is the power of weakness resolution. Stop
trying to get better at the things you suck at,
instead outsource to someone that is truly
exceptional and you too can become a lifelong
member of the 10X club.

CHAPTER 4

BUSINESS CONSTRUCTION

Develop success from failures. Discouragement and failure are two of the surest stepping stones to success. – **Dale Carnegie**

CHAPTER 4
BUSINESS CONSTRUCTION

Business Construction (BC)

During the Business Construction phase, we focus on three main areas:

- *We implement the Action Plan, which covers weakness resolution and drives opportunities.*

- We rigorously test all new tools, systems, technology, and marketing strategies.
- We monitor ROI on all marketing tactics in Beta test mode. It is crucial to test out marketing tactics before scaling so we do not waste much time, effort, and money. We aim to achieve a minimum 3x ROI on all marketing strategies but would prefer to stay in beta test mode until we can attain a 5x return on marketing dollars spent.

Imagine the BC phase as doing time in the minor leagues. You now have the fundamentals (your action plan), but you still need to hone your skills before you are ready for the big leagues.

Implementing your action plan may be one of the hardest parts of the entire process of reorganizing your business. Two main pitfalls derail most advisors at this stage.

1. Even though they have already admitted their weakness, they still have trouble letting go. I have seen it time and time again. Joe Smith Advisor understands that he is not exceptional at a particular facet of his business, but he is either too proud, or too unwilling to delegate to

systems, technology, or other people.

2. The other major pitfall is that the advisor just does not know how to solve the weakness.

The antidote for these problems is really quite simple.

1. Suck it up and repeat after me, "I cannot be good at everything." When you wake up each morning, make sure that those are the very first words that you utter. Trust me, it is really quite freeing. For most of us, it is a 180-degree shift in our mindset, but you cannot be a 10X'er until you understand yourself.

2. Once you have created your list of opportunities, find successful financial advisors that you admire and quiz them on how they are solving that piece of the puzzle.

An even better opportunity for success exists if you are willing to invest in your business. An excellent consultant can help save you a boatload of time and mistakes and help jump-start your path to stardom. Our consulting service at www.fa-mentor.com is a great example.

PLEASE keep in mind; the QLS program is a blueprint to help you build your successful business. It is not intended to fill in all the tactical details of how you run your biz. For example, a blueprint for building a house will tell you where the walls should go, but it does not specify what color those walls should be or what type of fixture should adorn the sinks or the tile that trims the hearth.

The same is true for your business. The QLS formula gives you the fundamental building blocks, while still allowing your personality to shine through. This system does not try to mandate the use of any single process or technology. It does not try to pigeonhole you into a particular way of doing business. For example, you have the flexibility to create your own client onboarding experience and client servicing model, along with just about every aspect of how you run your business.

The components to these experiences are far less important than the sheer fact that you have those processes institutionalized and dialed in. The model is flexible enough to work for anyone that has the desire, dedication and strength to want to be a better version of their current self. With all of that said, if you would like help to determine the "color of your walls,"

I highly suggest that you work with a consultant to help fill in some of the details.

The following is a good place to start your process: Create your Action Plan by listing all of your opportunities. Then create a simple short description of how you are going to implement a plan to exploit each opportunity. The following are a few examples:

Opportunity: I spend too much time managing my client's accounts and it takes me away from creating relationships and deepening relationships.

Solution: I am going to create five model portfolios across the risk continuum and fit all my clients into one of those five portfolios based on their risk profile. Or, utilize the services of a turnkey asset management program (TAMP), like www.sofosinvestments.com, and outsource the time, effort and frustration of managing money.

Opportunity: I meet a substantial number of prospects at the weekly seminars that I hold, but my close rate is too low.

Solution: Create an automated follow-up process so that attendees that do not commit to an appointment get put into a drip system so that you are top of mind when they are ready for your services. Start a monthly newsletter that provides the prospect with valuable information and positions you as the subject matter expert in your niche.

Opportunity: I am a great closer, but I cannot prospect for new clients to save my life.

Solution: Hire a junior advisor that is exceptional at driving new leads.

Opportunity: I am not getting any referrals.

Solution: Start surveying your clients quarterly so that you can better understand your clients' needs and increase your value proposition. Then create an automated campaign around continuously asking for referrals.

During the Business Construction Phase, it is paramount that you test, test, test, and then retest all of your new systems. You are going to be changing the vast majority of how you operate your business if you want to be a 10X advisor, and you need to make sure that you are ready for prime time when the money is on the line.

For example, let us say that you are going to

implement a new client onboarding system. Client onboarding is the process of bringing on a new client into your business. It is your opportunity to build a relationship, address concerns, ensure they understand the services available to them, get the client up to speed and start the relationship on the right foot. This process may be as simple as a checklist of items that your assistant does for each new client, or it could be built into an automated workflow within your CRM system.

Regardless of how you deliver this experience, it needs to be replicable and foolproof. This is your only chance to make a first impression, so there must be a zero margin for error. Whether it is client on-boarding, customer service, investment management, communication, or anything else, without a replicable process, there will be an error. 10X advisors eliminate the mistakes and confusion to deliver the best possible client experience, maintain their clients for life, and gather more referrals.

The final part of the Business Construction (BC) phase is the relentless and rigorous testing of your marketing tactics. Most 10X advisors want to attract new clients continuously. Therefore, the pursuit of new blood should definitely make your Action Plan. A common mistake that I see non-10X'ers make is jumping with both feet into the pool on each new shiny marketing idea that comes along. All 10X'ers have three things in common.

1. They start slow and test their marketing before they scale.

2. They diversify across several marketing tactics.

3. They relentlessly measure the ROI on their dollars invested.

Think back to our lessons learned from America's Fortune 500 companies. Can you imagine Microsoft running a full-scale advertisement campaign without beta testing it on a small segment of the market first? Can you imagine Microsoft having just one marketing tactic? Would you expect that Microsoft would know precisely how much money they get back for every dollar that they spend on every campaign? If Microsoft violated those three marketing truisms, they would not be the world's second-largest company. 10X advisors run their marketing like a business. They test before they scale. They diversify tactics to protect against over penetration and changing preferences. They know their numbers. If you do not know your return on investment, how can you possibly know where to deploy your limited resources?

CHAPTER 5

CONFIRMATION

What we really want to do is what we are really meant to do. When we do what we are meant to do, money comes to us, doors open for us, we feel useful, and the work we do feels like play to us. - Julia Cameron

CHAPTER 5
CONFIRMATION

In the Business construction phase, we implemented our Action Plan, rigorously tested our new systems and made sure that our beta test on our marketing was profitable. Now we are ready to turn up the heat and move to the next phase- Confirmation (C)

Confirmation (C)

Before we get started with the confirmation phase of our business planning, let us first take a look backward so we can see how far we have come. Looking at our mathematical equation,

$$ASN+CIN+SRN=QLSN$$
$$QLSN+WR+BMS*EX=QLS$$

You have created a full assessment of your strengths, weaknesses, and opportunities through a careful analysis of the total life cycle of client engagement and sales process **(ASN)**.

You have measured the amount of time you spend engaging with prospects and clients, versus the time spent on other activities that are not revenue-generating **(CIN)**.

You have taken a deep dive into all of the elements of your business that are necessary components to truly scale your business for massive and sustainable growth **(SRN)**.

By adding all three pieces together, you have your Quantum Leap Success Number **(QLSN)**, the foundation on which you can begin to build around.

Next, you built out a strategy for resolving all weaknesses uncovered during the evaluation phase (ASN + CIN + SRN), a process called weakness resolution **(WR)**.

You are now ready to work through the confirmatory phase of your findings.

In the Confirmation phase, we prove that you have a replicable model that is ready to scale and drive massive and sustainable growth. You should focus your attention on three main areas:

- Confirm that all implementations are working properly and firing on all cylinders.
- Diligently measure and chart your CIN monthly to confirm that you are spending your time most profitably.
- Replicate marketing tactics at a more aggressive rate to prove the sustainability of ROI.

Confirm that all implementations from your action plan are firing on all cylinders. At this point, you have implemented a plethora of new systems, technology, marketing tactics and possibly other people. The confirmation phase is your chance to stress test everything that you have built before you go big. Think of this stage as a dress rehearsal before the big opening night show. The first thing to consider during the confirmation phase is that perfection is not attainable.

When implementing sophisticated new

business processes, there is a learning curve. You will find outlier use cases that you had not planned for. You will have things that fail in unintended ways that you never considered. This is exactly why the confirmation phase is so important. Test, test, test, and then test again before allowing yourself to call this phase of the model complete. I have seen advisors stay in the confirmation phase for weeks, while other advisors take several months to get it right. Do not try to scale your business before you have your house in order. Take it slow and get it right and you will be well-equipped to build a business that will take you to the 10X-land.

The next step in the confirmation phase is to diligently measure and chart your CIN every month to confirm that you are spending your time most profitably. Up until this part in the process, you have been doing a substantial amount of non-revenue generating things to build out your business, with an eye on the future. Now it is time to start tracking your progress, or more explicitly tracking how you spend your time. In the evaluation phase, we created an initial baseline CIN score. The Client Interaction Number (CIN) measures the amount of time that you spend doing the things that make you money, creating relationships and deepening relationships. In other words, prospect and client-facing activities.

What percentage of your day do you spend doing prospect or client-facing activities? All too often, I see financial advisors work too hard and come away exhausted and still not find the results that they are looking for long-term. The truth is that we only get paid extremely well to do two things; create relationships and deepen relationships. Almost EVERYTHING else that we do is gross underemployment.

Earlier in this book, we reviewed the Rydex study regarding financial advisors' income levels based on the percentage of their time that they spent on prospect or client-facing activities. They found that advisors that spent more than 60% of their time creating relationships and deepening relationships made 8.42% times more money than their counterparts that spent 30% or less of their day on client-facing activities.

That is huge!!! In this confirmation phase, you should track everything that you do and assign a number of minutes to that task. Your goal is to be at 60% of your time, or greater spent with prospects and clients. The constant and diligent measurement of your CIN will give you powerful insights into all of the things that you are doing that are inhibiting your entry into the 10X club.

Here is a simple example of a tool used to measure your CIN.

A MENTOR
Advisor Name: _____

CLIENT INTERACTION NUMBER (CIN) QUESTIONNAIRE

Please provide the number of hours that you spend in a typical week doing the following activities:

Meeting with Clients: _____

Prospecting: _____

Everything Else: _____

Please list all activities and the hours per week you spend on the things that make up the "Everything Else" category from above.

Activity:	Hours per Wk.
Activity:	Hours per Wk.
Activity:	Hours per Wk.
Activity:	Hours per Wk.
Activity:	Hours per Wk.
Activity:	Hours per Wk.
Activity:	Hours per Wk.
Activity:	Hours per Wk.
Activity:	Hours per Wk.
Activity:	Hours per Wk.
Activity:	Hours per Wk.
Activity:	Hours per Wk.
Activity:	Hours per Wk.
Activity:	Hours per Wk.
Activity:	Hours per Wk.
Activity:	Hours per Wk.
Activity:	Hours per Wk.
Activity:	Hours per Wk.
Activity:	Hours per Wk.
Activity:	Hours per Wk.

Download the tool at www.fa-mentor.com

The next step in the confirmation phase is to replicate marketing tactics at a more aggressive rate to prove the sustainability of ROI. I have seen the absence of this step bite many financial advisors in the ass. Too often, an advisor finds a marketing tactic that works and then jumps in whole hog, just to find that his / her efforts weren't rewarded with a positive ROI.

During the Business Construction phase (BC), we tested marketing tactics on a very small scale to find the ones that produce a positive ROI. In the confirmation phase (C) we take the tactics that worked and turn up the heat.

- Spend more money on these programs and rigorously measure the results.
- Ensure that your initial small-scale test wasn't a fluke.
- Make sure that your marketing works at scale before you build a business model around it.
- Make sure that there isn't denigration in ROI as you spend more money and that you are maintaining at least a 3x return.
- It is crucial to keep in mind that marketing is the lifeblood of your business. Knowing how much money you put into the marketing machine and how much money will come back to you is absolutely imperative to run a successful business and scale it for massive and sustainable growth.

Wow, we have come a long way in the process to arrive at this point. You have stress-tested all systems and new technology, started tracking your CIN and tested your marketing tactics at scale for profitable ROI. Now it is time to get the party started and move into the Business Modeling & Scaling (BMS) phase of the game.

CHAPTER 6

BUSINESS MODELING

Money is only a tool. It will take you wherever you wish, but it will not replace you as the driver. - Ayn Rand

CHAPTER 6
BUSINESS MODELING

Business Modeling & Scaling (BMS)

In the Business Modeling and Scaling phase, you have now proven that you have a successful business model that is ready to scale. It is time to turn the crank and watch your business grow. In this phase, we will accomplish three tasks:

- You will implement a one-year marketing plan that details out everything that you are going to do during the year to drive business, with exacting specificity regarding timing and deliverables.

- You will create a one-year production goal plan that will measure the actual vs projected production monthly.
- You will have a complete Business Plan, which is the combination of your action plan, marketing plan, and production goals.

What is a marketing plan, and why do I need one?

A marketing plan is an operational document that outlines an advertising strategy that an organization will implement to generate leads and reach its target market. A marketing plan details the campaigns to be undertaken over a period, including how the company will measure the effect of these initiatives. A marketing plan can be either extremely complex or very basic.

At one point in my career, I paid an outside consultant over 20k to produce a marketing plan for my business. Wow, the output was a masterpiece. The plan was close to 250 pages long, and the binder was beautifully designed. Everything was spelled out in perfect specificity. Upon first reading, it made me feel like all warm and fuzzy inside as if I could rule the world if I followed the plan. I was positive that this marketing plan was going to be the difference-maker and send our business into the stratosphere. Guess what happened next? Wait for it----- the plan ended up being a total flop. It was a complete bust. Boy, oh boy, was that a great lesson.

If you have adequately completed each phase outlined within this book, your marketing plan should really be quite simple. Before I provide you with a really great and simple plan, let us explore why my 20k plan failed.

The first reason my 20k plan failed was that it was too complex. There was just too much to do and too much to implement. To utilize this plan properly, I would have needed several people with much more domain experience than we had available. The second reason the project failed is that the marketing strategies had not been tested. The consultant went through excruciating pain to research every single aspect of the target market. The consultant outlined all the demographics and details.

The plan was very well-thought-out on paper, but in the real world, nothing beats a real-life test. As we talked about in earlier chapters, start with a very small test. Make sure that you get an acceptable ROI. Crank up the volume and test it again. Marketing is a finicky animal. A marketing tactic may work great in one geographic region and fail in another. A marketing tactic may work great for one person and fail for another. Test, test, test, and test again. Here is a very effective and simple marketing plan that will propel you one step closer to the 10X club.

Here is a simple example of a tool used to create your marketing plan.

AMENTOR

Advisor Name: _____

MARKETING TACTIC DETAILS QUESTIONAIRRE

Marketing Tactic 1:
Name of Marketing Tactic: _____
Target Market: _____
Spend per Marketing Run: _____
Goal per Marketing Run: _____
Marketing Runs per Year: _____
Annual Spend: _____
Annual Goal: _____

Marketing Tactic 2:
Name of Marketing Tactic: _____
Target Market: _____
Spend per Marketing Run: _____
Goal per Marketing Run: _____
Marketing Runs per Year: _____
Annual Spend: _____
Annual Goal: _____

Marketing Tactic 3:
Name of Marketing Tactic: _____
Target Market: _____
Spend per Marketing Run: _____
Goal per Marketing Run: _____
Marketing Runs per Year: _____
Annual Spend: _____
Annual Goal: _____

Marketing Tactic 4:
Name of Marketing Tactic: _____
Target Market: _____
Spend per Marketing Run: _____
Goal per Marketing Run: _____
Marketing Runs per Year: _____
Annual Spend: _____
Annual Goal: _____

Marketing Tactic 5:
Name of Marketing Tactic: _____
Target Market: _____
Spend per Marketing Run: _____
Goal per Marketing Run: _____
Marketing Runs per Year: _____
Annual Spend: _____
Annual Goal: _____

Marketing Tactic 6:
Name of Marketing Tactic: _____
Target Market: _____
Spend per Marketing Run: _____
Goal per Marketing Run: _____
Marketing Runs per Year: _____
Annual Spend: _____
Annual Goal: _____

A MENTOR

Advisor Name: _____

MARKETING CALENDAR

A MENTOR	Date	Tactic Name	$ Spend	$ Result	ROI
January					
February					
March					
April					
May					
June					
July					
August					

Download the tool at www.fa-mentor.com

This plan consists of two parts:

1. a list of your marketing tactics details, and 2. your marketing calendar. Your list of marketing tactics should provide for the details of each marketing tactic that you will utilize.

For example, the name of your marketing tactic, your target market, the spend per marketing run, the number of marketing runs per year, your annual spend, and your annual goal per tactic. Here is an example of what this might look like:

Name of Marketing Tactic: Retirement Planning Dinner Seminar

Target market: 55 yrs. to 65 yrs. of age with 250k of investments

Spend per marketing run: $6500

Goal per marketing run: $30,000

Marketing runs per year: 12
(one a month)

Annual spend: $78,000

Annual goal: $360,000

Rinse, water, repeat. Do this exact same thing

for each marketing tactic that you plan to utilize during the year.

The second part of your simple marketing plan is your Marketing Calendar. My suggestion is that in December, you plan your marketing calendar for the entire next year. You can use a simple format like this:

Here is a simple example of a tool used to create your marketing calendar.

Download the tool at www.fa-mentor.com

In your marketing calendar, we are looking for

five key data points: date, tactic name, spend, results, ROI. This format has three primary purposes. First, it keeps you organized and helps you stay true to your plan. Second, it helps you measure your results. Every time you get a new client, look to your CRM and find the campaign that they came from and update the results field. Third, the continuous measurement of ROI will help you make informed decisions when the next December rolls around and you plan for the following year.

Your marketing tactics page will tell you which tactics you will use during the year, and your marketing calendar will detail when you are going to use them, how much you are going to spend and help you track the return of your marketing investment.

Now that you have completed your marketing plan, the heavy lifting is done, and creating your One Year Production Goal is a cinch. See the following example of a one-year production goal.

Here is a simple example of a tool used to

create your One-year Production Goal.

A MENTOR			Advisor Name:	
ONE YEAR PRODUCTION GOAL				
A MENTOR	Goal	Actual	Delta	% Delta
January				
February				
March				
April				
May				
June				
July				
August				
September				
October				
November				
December				

Download the tool at www.fa-mentor.com

Your production goals consist of your monthly goal and the actual production you accomplish for each month. Your monthly production goal can be calculated by going back to your marketing plan. On your Marketing Calendar, look at each marketing tactic that you plan to run during the month. Go to your Marketing Tactics Details sheet and match it with the "Goal Per Run," and add all the numbers together, then add your estimated base production from your current book of business. For example, in January, you planned three marketing tactics that you expected to return a total of 50k in production. Also, your current book of business produces about 40k per month in fees. You add the 50k that you planned on producing to the 40k in fees that you receive from your clients and the result is a 90k January production goal. Do the same for each month of the year.

Guess what, future 10X'ers? Your business plan is done. The combination of your action plan, your marketing plan, and your goals make up your business plan for the next year. Please keep in mind that this is not a one and done exercise. A 10x'er starts every new year with a new plan. Figure out what you did right, what you did wrong, and where your opportunities are for improvement. A 10X'er strives to get better at running their business every year by taking what they have learned and utilizing that wisdom for greater success.

CHAPTER 7

EXECUTION and ACCOUNTABILITY

You can only become truly accomplished at something you love. Don't make money your goal. Instead, pursue the things you love doing, and then do them so well that people can't take their eyes off you. - Maya Angelou

CHAPTER 7
EXECUTION and
ACCOUNTABILITY

Now that we have our business plan in place, it is time to move on to our final to stages, Execution (EX) and Accountability (A).

Execution (EX)

Before we get started with the execution and accountability phases of our business planning, let us first take a look back at our journey thus far — looking at our mathematical equation,

$$ASN+CIN+SRN=QLSN$$
$$QLSN+WR+BMS*EX= QLS$$

You have created a full assessment of your strengths, weaknesses, and opportunities through a careful analysis of the total life cycle of client engagement and sales process **(ASN)**.

You have measured the amount of time you spend engaging with prospects and clients, versus the time spent on other activities that are not revenue-generating **(CIN)**.

You have taken a deep dive into all of the elements of your business that are necessary components to truly scale your business for massive and sustainable growth **(SRN)**.

By adding all three pieces together, you have your Quantum Leap Success Number **(QLSN),** the foundation in which you can begin to build around.

Next, you built out a strategy for resolving all of the weaknesses uncovered during the evaluation phase (ASN + CIN + SRN), a process called weakness resolution **(WR)**.

You built out a scalable business model and documented it in a one-year business plan **(BMS)**.

Accountability (A)

Now for the final piece of the equation, execution **(EX)**.

The Execution phase is where the rubber hits the road. The best business model in the world will fail without accurate and diligent execution. Your success depends on your desire and ability to follow the model and not deviate from what has proven to be successful. If you have followed the process thus far, it is literally impossible to fail unless you do not execute.

Here are the three most common reasons why an advisor will never find their ticket punched to the 10X dance.

1. They have too much success too quickly. This sounds crazy, right? Unfortunately, too many advisors fall into the trap of thinking that they are smarter than the plan. They start out following the plan and have some initial success and then

believe that their success was based on the brilliance of their personality, not the rigor of a well laid out business model. Sadly, they end up going back to their past tendencies and abandon everything that they have learned.

2. The next most prevalent reason for failure is the exact opposite of the reason above. The advisor gets off to a slow start and loses belief in the process without giving it a chance to let it work. This movie generally plays out like this: The advisor starts marketing campaign number one from his / her marketing calendar and the results come back sub-par. Advisor then cancels the next campaign. The advisor waits and waits to see if some of the stragglers from the first campaign come to fruition. Months later, the advisor runs a second campaign and still achieves mediocre results. The advisor then throws up their hands and declares the venture a failure. This advisor failed because of a straightforward error; they didn't follow their marketing calendar. Marketing takes time and practice. As with everything in life the more you do it, the better you get. Not all campaigns work the same. You can run the exact same

marketing tactic and get totally different results because of the month, season, weather, economic factors, and/or a million other reasons. Keep in mind that a sample size of one is not statistically significant. Remember that when you get down on yourself because of one bad result, you need to pick yourself up and keep fighting. You win with marketing when you have a plan and stick to your plan religiously. You fail when you deviate.

3. Another reason advisors fail is that they stop tracking their **CIN**. Remember the Client Interaction Number (CIN) measures the amount of time that you spend doing the things that actually make you money, creating relationships and deepening relationships. In other words, prospect and client-facing activities. Rydex source proved that financial advisors' income levels are based on the percentage of their time that they spent on prospect or client-facing activities. They found that advisors that spent more than 60% of their time creating relationships and deepening relationships made 8.4 times more money than their counterparts that spent 30% or less of their day on client-facing activities. The

10X advisor relentlessly measures and documents every minute spent interacting with prospects and clients and chart it weekly. If that number is south of sixty percent of your entire workweek, you are leaving money on the table.

If you want to be a 10X'er do not fall into the trap of the mediocre. You built a sound business model. You tested it every step of the way. You documented your business model, strategy, and tactics within a business plan. Now stick to the plan, do not deviate and watch the magic happen.

Now that we all understand the importance of execution, let us remember that we are human, and unfortunately, that condition comes with certain frailties. From time to time, we tend to get down on ourselves and revert to bad habits. The best way to fight the human condition is to find a coach that will hold you accountable. Okay, I know what you are thinking. Probably something like, "I have been in this business for twenty years, why the heck do I need a coach?" Keep in mind, almost every professional athlete has a coach. Professional golfers have a swing coach to make sure that they do not slip into bad habits. NFL quarterbacks have a throwing coach to ensure that their throwing motion and footwork move in the proper sequence. A coach is there to help you reach your maximum potential. You should have a coach to make sure that you stay true to your course, you do not regress into bad habits, and to pick you up when you get down on yourself. Your coach should help you with the following:

- Create a culture of measuring key business metrics. You should be held responsible for having your numbers updated weekly. It is crucially important to focus on the areas that drive success.
- Constantly evaluate your ROI and adjust your marketing tactics as needed.
- Make sure that you are religiously following all aspects of your business plan.
- Track and monitor your CIN, to assure that you are spending your time doing the things that drive massive growth.
- Keep your mood positive. This is one of the hardest things to do in

the business world. It is easy to get frustrated, or down on yourself. Keep a smile on your face, work hard with a good attitude and you will find the truth that you are looking for.

CHAPTER 8
THE 10X CLUB

Innovation distinguishes between a leader and a follower. - Steve Jobs

CHAPTER 8
THE 10X CLUB

Welcome to The 10X Club

At the beginning of the book, I gave you the simple equation:

$$(ASN+CIN+SRN=QLSN$$
$$QLSN+WR+BMS*EX= QLS)$$

and promised that it would eventually make sense. Let us recap.

You have created a full assessment of your strengths, weaknesses, and opportunities through a careful analysis of the total life cycle of client engagement and sales process **(ASN)**.

You have measured the amount of time you spend engaging with prospects and clients, versus the time spent on other activities that are not revenue-generating **(CIN)**.

You have taken a deep dive into all of the elements of your business that are necessary components to truly scale your business for massive and sustainable growth **(SRN)**.

By adding all three pieces together, you have your Quantum Leap Success Number **(QLSN)**, the foundation on which you can begin to build.

Next, you built out a strategy for resolving all of the weaknesses uncovered during the evaluation phase (ASN + CIN + SRN), a process call weakness resolution **(WR)**.

You built out a scalable business model and documented it in a one-year business plan **(BMS)**.

You busted your hump, did all the right things, and followed your business plan religiously. This all culminated in the Capstone and final piece of the equation, execution **(EX)**.

You add up all the pieces of this equation and you get your **(QLS)** Quantum Leap Success. The Quantum Leap Success formula was created to give you a path to massive and sustainable growth. As with any blueprint, there is a great deal of latitude in what the final product looks like. A blueprint to build a house will tell you where the walls should go, but it does not specify what color those walls should be. The same is true for your business. The QLS formula gives you the fundamental building blocks, while still allowing your personality to shine through. We do not try to mandate the use of any single process or technology. We do not try to pigeonhole you into a certain way of doing business. For example, you have the flexibility to create your own client onboarding experience and client servicing model. The components of these experiences are far less important than the sheer fact that you have those processes institutionalized and dialed in. The model is flexible to work for anyone that has the desire, dedication and strength to want to be a better version of their current self.

You are now in possession of the blueprint that will allow you to transform your practice and turn it into a thriving and sustainable business. You can be the one in your company that everyone else is envious of and looks up to. You possess the knowledge to accomplish the very pinnacle of success within financial services. You can become a card-carrying member of the 10X club. Now, it is your move, what are you going to do?

ABOUT THE AUTHOR

Scott Winters has had a successful multi-decade career in the financial services industry as a top financial advisor, manager and executive. Notable accomplishments are that he built a wealth management business from zero to over two billion in assets managed across over 20,000 clients. He co-founded, built and sold one of the fastest-growing wealth management businesses in America (according to Forbes).

As a CEO, he has managed and inspired hundreds of employees. Scott is a widely recognized speaker, author, entrepreneur, and leader. He has mentored, managed, or trained thousands of financial advisors and helped them achieve greater success.

Scott has continuously rewritten the book on the use of technology and practice management disciplines to help achieve massive and sustainable business growth. He is an active board member for several companies and an angel investor. Scott has a BA in Business Economics from San Diego State University. Scott holds the following licenses, series 7, 24, 63, 65 and Texas life & Health. He is also a Chartered Retirement Planning Counselor, CRPC.

To contact Scott or for more information, visit:

www.fa-mentor.com

INDEX

Advisor Success Number, vii, 3, 5, 90

Advisor Success Number (ASN), 3, 5

Business Modeling, vii, 117, 119

CIN = Client Interaction Number, 3

client appreciation events, 19, 67

Client onboarding, 55, 106

client servicing model, 7, 19, 57, 58, 59, 104, 143

confirmation phase, 110, 112, 113, 114, 115, 116

crucial elements of designing your market, 28

customer value, 21

DAS, 15, 16

Delusional Activity Syndrome, 15

Diagnostics phase, 90

Execution, vii, 130, 134

Execution phase, 134

FA Mentor Coaching, 90

firing clients, 19, 78

getting referrals, 19, 60, 61

Life Cycle of Client Engagement, 5

managing your client's investments, 19, 76

marketing, 4, 9, 18, 19, 25, 26, 27, 29, 36, 37, 39, 40, 41, 42, 43, 45, 46, 47, 48, 49, 50, 61, 62, 64, 86, 96, 102, 107, 108, 110, 112, 115, 116, 117, 119, 120, 121, 122, 124, 125, 126, 127, 128, 135, 139, 149

mission, 18, 20, 21, 22, 30, 32, 47, 55, 82

mission statement, 18, 20, 21, 22, 30

multi-generational client retention, 19, 63, 65

multi-pronged
marketing plan, 19,
49
Net Promoter Score, 19,
51
Niche marketing, 27
Quantum Leap Success
Number (QLSN), 4,
90, 111, 131, 142
ROI, 18, 40, 50, 102,
108, 112, 115, 116,
117, 121, 126, 139

Scale Ready Number,
vii, 3, 16, 90
software, 35
target customer, 24, 27
The 10X Club, 141
The Quantum Leap
Success Formula, vi,
ix
value proposition, 18,
20, 21, 22, 30, 38, 47,
52, 85, 86, 106
Weakness Resolution,
vii, 95, 96

REFERENCES PAGE

Coca Cola Source:
https://www.forbes.com/sites/greatspeculations/2019/03/13/can-coca-cola-increase-its-revenue-and-profitability-by-slashing-its-advertising-the-next-two-years/#383396a44196

Ganter Source:
https://www.gartner.com/smarterwithgartner/gartner-cmo-spend-survey-2016-2017-shows-marketing-budgets-continue-to-climb/

Demand Network Source:
https://www.demandmetric.com/content/content-marketing-infographic

Content Marketing Institute Source:
https://contentmarketinginstitute.com/2015/10/b2c-content-marketing-research/

Arris Source:
https://blogs.wsj.com/cmo/2014/05/28/why-the-c3-v-c7-debate-in-tv-advertising-may-be-irrelevant/

Boomers Source:
https://www.marketingcharts.com/uncategorize
d-22891

Investment News Survey:
http://www.investmentnews.com/article/201507
13/FEATURE/150719999/the-great-wealth-
transfer-is-coming-putting-advisers-at-risk

Accenture Source:
https://www.accenture.com/us-
en/~/media/accenture/conversion-
assets/dotcom/documents/global/pdf/industries_
5/accenture-cm-awams-wealth-transfer-final-
june2012-web-version.pdf

SCOTT WINTERS

Made in the USA
Columbia, SC
26 October 2023

25002898R00096